W9-CDH-824

THE REFERENCE
INTERVIEW TODAY

THE REFERENCE INTERVIEW TODAY

Susan Knoer

LIBRARIES UNLIMITED LIBRARY MANAGEMENT COLLECTION

Gerard B. McCabe, Series Editor

 **LIBRARIES UNLIMITED**

AN IMPRINT OF ABC-CLIO, LLC
Santa Barbara, California • Denver, Colorado • Oxford, England

Library of Congress Cataloging-in-Publication Data

Knoer, Susan.
    The reference interview today / Susan Knoer.
        p. cm. — (The Libraries Unlimited library management collection)
    Includes bibliographical references and index.
    ISBN 978–1–59884–822–9 (alk. paper) — ISBN 978-1–59884–823–6 (ebook)
    1. Reference services (Libraries) 2. Electronic reference services (Libraries) 3. Reference librarians—Effect of technological innovations on. I. Title.
Z711.K57   2011
025.5′2—dc22   2011010354

ISBN: 978–1–59884–822–9
EISBN: 978–1–59884–823–6

15 14 13 12 11   1 2 3 4 5

This book is also available on the World Wide Web as an eBook.
Visit www.abc-clio.com for details.

Libraries Unlimited
An Imprint of ABC-CLIO, LLC

ABC-CLIO, LLC
130 Cremona Drive, P.O. Box 1911
Santa Barbara, California 93116-1911

This book is printed on acid-free paper ∞

Manufactured in the United States of America

CONTENTS

INTRODUCTION: YOU DON'T HAVE TO LEARN IT (ALL) AGAIN

THE HISTORY OF THE REFERENCE INTERVIEW

We are challenged to meet our users at their point of need. That's not easy since the library has never been their only point of need, and face-to-face is no longer the only way of conducting the reference interview. Our users are many and everywhere, and we are few and often anchored to our collections.

We must change our location both physically and virtually to give them the services we promise. Reference is the heart of library service, and the reference interview is the heart of reference. The actual interview has changed little, but the environment has changed vastly.

In researching this book, I ran across *Reference Services Today: From Interview to Burnout* (Katz and Fraley 1987). In their opening words, they lament the declining budgets, overworked librarians, and encroaching automation and disintermediation. That isn't a surprise, except that this book came out in 1987. There are some things that are constant in our profession; our big constant is change. Computers didn't change everything, but they changed the way we do most things.

The history of the reference interview in the library literature is fairly short. It undoubtedly was in use before anyone wrote about it. It's a natural part of our experience working in the library, but it has been written down so that we don't have to learn by experimenting every day. The following statements will sound familiar to librarians today:

"When scholars and persons of high social position come to a library, they have confidence enough, in regard to the cordiality of their reception, to make known their wishes without timidity or reserve. Modest men in the humbler walks of life, and well-trained boys and girls, need encouragement before they become ready to say freely what they want.

"A hearty reception by a sympathizing friend and the recognition of someone at hand who will listen to inquiries, even although he may consider them unimportant, make it easy for such persons to ask questions and put them at once on home footing.

"A school-boy calls for a history of the Suez Canal. You see at once, probably that what he needs is a brief account, and refer him to some recently-issued encyclopaedia. At the same time you show him how to use dictionaries and encyclopaedias, and tell him he can often find answers to questions himself by works of this kind, but invite him to you whenever he encounters snags or fails to get the information sought after.

"Another business man wishes for certain statistics of trade, manufactures, and inventions. He has no time to spare in collecting the books he desires. He does not know how to get hold of them so well as a librarian does.

" 'Isn't the sentence, "God tempers the wind to the shorn lamb," in the Bible?' asks another. The librarian answers, "No" and refers for further information to Bartlett's 'Familiar Quotations.'

"A board of trade is discussing the question of the advisableness of introducing the metric system of weights and measures into common use. Members call upon librarians to furnish the best treatises on the subject.

"A librarian is frequently asked to give information in regard to things and processes which he knows nothing about. Perhaps he is called upon to produce a description of an object the name of which is unknown to him. I remember slyly consulting a dictionary to find out what a 'cam' is, and again for the definition of 'link-valve motion.'

"But having acquired a definite notion of the object concerning which information is desired, the habit of mental classification, which a librarian acquires so readily, comes to his aid.

"There are obvious limits to the assistance which a librarian can undertake to render. Common-sense will dictate them. Thus no librarian would take the responsibility of recommending books to give directions for the treatment of disease. Nor would he give legal advice nor undertake to instruct applicants in regard to the practical manipulations of the workshop or laboratory.

"I need not remind you, however, that many persons who use a library have to be instructed in regard to the use of catalogues, and need practice before they can use them to the best advantage.

"But the time is distant when the whole field of knowledge can be covered by these notes; and even when it shall be occupied, much personal assistance will still be needed by readers in popular libraries.

"Of course, too, it will always be necessary for a librarian to extend to readers the hospitalities of his institution.

"Among the good results which attend personal intercourse on the part of the librarian with users of popular libraries, the following may be mentioned.

"*First.* If you gain the respect and confidence of readers, and they find you easy to get at and pleasant to talk with, great opportunities are afforded of stimulating the love of study and of directing investigators to the best sources of information.

"*Second.* You find out what books the actual users of the library need, and your judgment improves in regard to the kind of books it is best to add to it. You see what subjects the constituency of the institution are interested in, and what is the degree of simplicity they require in the presentation of knowledge.

"*Third.* One of the best means of making a library *popular* is to mingle freely with its users, and help them in every way. When this policy is pursued for a series of years in any town, a very large portion of the citizens receive answers to questions, and the conviction spreads through the community that the library is an institution of such beneficent influences that it can not be dispensed with.

"*Fourth, and last.* The collections of books which make up the contents of the circulating departments of our libraries have been provided for the use of persons of differing degrees of refinement and moral susceptibility, and for those who occupy mental planes of various altitudes.

"Place in the circulating department one of the most accomplished persons in the corps of your assistants. . . . Instruct this assistant to consult with every person who asks for help in selecting books. This should not be her whole work; for work of this kind is best done when it has the *appearance* of being performed incidentally. Let the assistant, then, have some regular work, but such employment as she can at once lay aside when her aid is asked for in picking out books to read.

"Six years ago I was a member of the Board of Directors of the Free Public Library of the city of Worcester, Massachusetts. At that time I noticed that its reference department was hardly used at all and was fast becoming an unpopular institution. During the last five or six years, by the adoption of the means recommended in this paper, a large use of this department has grown up, and it has come to be highly appreciated in the community.

"A librarian should be as unwilling to allow an inquirer to leave the library with his question unanswered as a shop-keeper is to have a customer go out of his store without making a purchase.

"In personal intercourse with readers, there are certain mental tendencies which should be restrained. Idle curiosity is one of them. Many scholars prefer to pursue their studies privately, and are annoyed if they think they are observed.

"Respect reticence. If you approach a reader with the purpose of aiding him, and find him unwilling to admit you to his confidence, regard his wishes and allow him to make investigations by himself.

"Avoid scrupulously the propagation of any particular set of views in politics, art, history, philosophy, or theology.

"The more freely a librarian mingles with readers, and the greater the amount of assistance he renders them, the more intense does the conviction of citizens, also, become, that the library is a useful institution, and the more willing do they grow to grant money in larger and larger sums to be used in buying books and employing additional assistants."

That sounds like sound contemporary advice. It's from Green's (1876) "Personal Relations between Librarians and Readers," published in the American Library Journal. It is the first published article on reference services. The entire article is worth reading since changing the word "mail" to "e-mail" would make it as applicable now as it was then.

The roots of what we do in all of reference are there and probably had been for some time before they were written down. They still apply. Roving reference, ethics, children's reference, information literacy, ready reference, readers' advisory, the seeds of Ranganathan's laws—they are all there. But read the first statement again: "need encouragement before they become ready to say freely what they want." There is the birth of the reference interview, if not in fact, at least in print.

To put it in context, Green talks about retraining his reference department six years before, in 1870. This article, which was delivered at the first American Library Association meeting, appeared more than 10 years before the first library science program was established at Columbia University in 1887.

We use the same skills that have been used for more than a hundred years, but we do not have the luxury of spending decades learning them, nor do our patrons, who want fast, efficient service. Reference is a service industry.

QUESTIONS FOR REFERENCE LIBRARIANS

Why do we need the reference interview? It is the heart of reference. If you know all the technology and sources but not what patrons are really asking, you'll give them good answers to the wrong questions. Of course, if you have terrific interview skills but don't know where to find the answer, you will be very pleasant but not very effective. You need both skill sets, but the people skills are the hardest to learn.

You may feel intimidated and overwhelmed by all the new stuff: texting, tweets, avatars, and all the rest. Get used to it, as there will be more new stuff to come. There always is. The good news is that they all use the same skill sets, just in a different setting. Once you know how to do it, it's simply a matter of learning the latest "how-to" or "where-to."

We want to meet the user at his point of need. Today, that may be as an avatar on the Second Life Web site, on one's cell phone in the woods, or in the classroom. Wherever a patron needs help, that's where we should be. For public libraries, that's where the public is; there should at least be posters and bookmarks that tell people that we help. Even better is to talk to local schools, businesses, and governmental agencies and ask if they will put a link on their site. For academic libraries, that may be quick-response codes on campus and embedded librarians in the course management system. For special libraries and archives, that may be a librarian on-site for openings of exhibits and conferences. The point of need may be anywhere; we need to be everywhere we can.

That's easier said than done. Who will monitor the Second Life library, the tweets, the instant messaging account, the e-mail, the Facebook page, the podcasts, the blog, and all the cool new technologies while the librarian does the things librarians traditionally do? Reference interviews take time, often a great deal of it. We need allies within the library and within the community.

We need the reference interview to find out exactly what the patron needs. That's the big difference between librarians and search engines. Google will give you everything. A reference librarian will give you just what you need. We are the original search engines—and the best ones. We can even work when the power is out.

Our job is translate the poorly framed question based on a vague information need into something that we or they can use to find the information that satisfies that need. We translate concepts into usable information. We translate that information into an answer to the question. That's a large enough task, and we shouldn't have to translate the answer for the patron too. We shouldn't make the patron do the translation back into understandable language. That's part of our job: to give a usable answer in plain language.

While we are free to our patrons, we do have our costs. Besides payroll, there are barriers we have to overcome. Some are technological, and some we have built for ourselves.

There are some basic truths we must remember as librarians. Patrons are not librarians. Not everyone understands machine-readable cataloging, Library of Congress, or Dewey classification or subject headings. In fact, only librarians and serious researchers do. Nor do others care. Patrons don't realize that not everything is online, that not everything is free online, that what is on the Web is not reliable or up to date, or that the librarian won't do all the research for them. Patrons don't know that everyone who works in a library isn't a librarian or that librarians do more than read all day.

Patrons do not know that the online public access catalog (OPAC) is not Google Books, that they can't get always full text (except when it's an online book), or that all databases aren't full text or what an index is. We need to help them—and often teach them—what we learned in graduate school.

Patrons think we *know* the answer, especially for ready reference questions. They think of us as encyclopedias, not as search engines.

Patrons think that we spend out days either reshelving books or sitting at a desk reading. We're surrounded by books, so we read. How hard can we work?

So let's take on some misconceptions from our side, one at a time:

"Avoid jargon": Better than that, let's just wipe it out. Jargon is the "secret language" of a group. It may be slang, it may be technical in the case of doctors, and it may not mean what it sounds like, in the case of lawyers' "terms of art." In the case of librarians, it's our own vocabulary, one that no one else understands. We can use it among ourselves, but there's no reason to inflict it on our patrons. When we use it, we have to explain it to the patron, so why use it outside our community? Here are a few examples.

"Circulation": I cringe every time I see that sign. Are they doing medical tests there? How about "Checkout"? That's pretty straightforward, and we've all seen it in retail stores. We get it.

"OPAC": Didn't we deal with them in the last oil crisis? "Online catalog" is much more user friendly, or just "catalog": many of our users don't know we ever had a paper catalog. Many of our librarians don't either.

"Information": That's what we go to libraries for, right? But the information desk isn't likely to help you buy a safe car or find a parking place. How about "Answers"?

"Reference": Yes, we love that term, but it doesn't mean much to others. We answer questions. How about "Questions" or the international symbol of the question mark? That may be simplistic, but we need to find a better way to tell patrons what we do.

"Negotiating the question": While it was intended in the sense of negotiating rough seas or tight passages, most of us think about negotiating a deal. We don't want to negotiate the question that way at all. We don't want to twist the question to fit an answer we already know or to ignore the real question to answer one that is more acceptable to us. We want to understand the true question.

Libraries may be the victims of their own success. As information literacy becomes more integrated into college classes, students become more independent. As public libraries provide more computers on-site with live librarians at hand, patrons become more independent. As more users have computers at home, smart phones, netbooks, and other connections, they have more options to find information on their own.

What that means is that we get the more of the harder questions and fewer of the quick and easy ones. Remember that when you complain about the directional questions you get some days.

The reference interview is at the heart of our services. It is the value-added proposition for libraries. Wherever and whenever we do it, we need to do it well. We need to brand ourselves as the "answer people." We are the reference librarians, and that's what we do.

Much of what I have written here was learned from years of work at reference desks in libraries and archives, working with patrons of all types and ages and answering questions via many media. Much of it is common sense to those with experience, but common sense is often taught through experience and not library science programs. As we depend more on paraprofessionals and staff and as new librarians join the profession, we need to codify that commonsense knowledge. What used to be passed on by word of mouth now needs to be in a concrete form to share with our many allies in the library.

For those who want more information, history, and theory, further reading is given for each chapter. For every reference situation, there is much more to learn, but much of it is specific to one situation. Explore the readings, use the forms, and try the tutorials. You may never tweet, but you'll have a resource to fall back on if you do, and you won't feel ignorant when someone mentions it. What you will use every day will be the reference interview in all its forms.

REFERENCES

Green, Samuel Swets. "Personal Relations between Librarians and Readers." *American Library Journal* 1 (1876): 74–81.
Katz, William, and Ruth Fraley. *Reference Services Today: From Interview to Burnout.* New York: Haworth, 1987.

1 REFERENCE FACE-TO-FACE

Why do we do what we do? Why is the reference interview necessary when the patron has already asked his question? We'll go into details later, but the most important one is Ranganathan's (1931) fourth law: save the reader's time. That's where our value lies: in helping the patron find what he needs. There is a flip side to that, however, in that the reference interview saves the librarian's time. When librarians have more and more tasks on their plates and a long line of patrons at the desk, getting to the core of the question and answering it saves precious time.

We call it the reference interview and not "answering the question" for a reason. The first question the patron asks is usually not his real question. Answering that inquiry first, without finding out the details, will rarely give the patron the information he needs. The patron is asking you because he doesn't know how to find the information himself. That means he doesn't know what to ask for, how to phrase it, or even if it exists. The reference interview defines the types and scope of information the patron needs. The reference interview, first and foremost, is analytical. We analyze the patron's question in terms of what he really needs, not just what he asked for.

It also helps us. It identifies gaps in our collections and knowledge. If the patron asks for something that we can't answer from our collections or for a format we don't know, it lets us know where we need to work. Keeping good records of what we can't do will help us prioritize training and purchase decisions.

SEEING YOURSELF AS OTHERS DO

Libraries are strange territory to people, even people who have used them before. If you grew up using the children's department, the adult sections were scary and forbidden. If you are used to public libraries and the Dewey Decimal

System, a large academic library using Library of Congress classification will be intimidating.

Reference, from the patron's point of view, is walking up to a stranger and asking where a good restaurant is in a strange town. It's intimidating: you don't know if you'll be ignored or if the answer will be correct. You have to trust the answer you're given, so you look for someone who looks like they belong there and who looks friendly or maybe someone who makes eye contact with you. You feel insecure and vulnerable when you have to ask for help, as you feel like you're imposing on them.

That's what librarians should look like: friendly helpful people who know what they're doing. If you don't, the rest of what you learn will be wasted. That's why patrons are satisfied with reference services that don't give them an answer, when the librarian is friendly. If the first encounter is pleasant, they will come back. Librarians tend to center on getting the right answer more than the relationship with the patron and vice versa. Never think of the patron as the problem (even if he is). The patron is your customer. Don't let your attitude get in the way

To many patrons, you are an authority figure—and not in a good way. You represent an institution. For many people, institutions are things like police, doctors, and the military: people who are supposed to help you but who you don't question. That's true especially for people from other cultures and countries. How are you going to change that perception?

MODELS OF PATRON SERVICE

Practice thinking of yourself in a retail setting. After all, what we're doing is customer service. Think of shopping for a dog. You go to the pet store and say you want a dog. Would you take the first dog that someone showed you? Or would you ask questions? What breed is it (paper or online)? How old is it? What's its pedigree (authoritative or anonymous)? Is it good with kids (user level)? It's not likely that you walk in knowing that you want a two-year-old black peekapoo that likes cats, doesn't bark, and is paper trained. Well, maybe you knew you wanted some of that.

If you don't like the retail model, think of the doctor-patient model. The patient doesn't know what's wrong; he knows only symptoms and vague terms. The doctor knows how to find out and fix it but only with your help. You want the doctor to ask questions, to follow with more questions, and to listen to you. You want him to talk to you in plain language, not in medical terms you don't understand. After all, if you knew what was wrong and what to do, you wouldn't be there. You want the doctor to explain what he's doing and why, when you'll get results, and what follow-up there will be, and you want him to do it with a smile to allay the anxiety (Radcliff 1995).

People will ask for a book about new cars, but the best information may be in an article or online. They may ask for the book about archaeologists in the

Middle East around the turn of the century but neglect to say it's fiction. They may ask for the "number mysteries" by Janet Evanovich but mean the "alphabet mysteries" by Sue Grafton. People will ask for a book that's on reserve but that's really on hold. It's your job to translate that into something you can use to search, not the patron's. If the patron knew how to do it himself, he would. Most patrons will if they have even a slight idea of how to. Patrons who are asking you really do need your help and are asking for it.

They ask in the best way they know. They have no idea of what we need to help them, so they may phrase their question too broadly (I need a book on mammals) or too narrowly (I need a book on grooming white Persian kittens for a 10-year-old) or get the details wrong. That's why we have the reference interview.

Why do people rely on friends and family for information and not libraries? They are taught to listen to their parents and family as children, when they are dependent on them. Family and friends are trusted. They are available. They ask you questions about why you need information and answer your questions in context. They will talk you through the process. They will show you how to do things. What's not to like?

Can we say as much about the reference desk? Often not. We are understaffed and overworked as more and more media and online sources are added every day but staffing levels drop.

Libraries are often the last place people come to for information. They try the easy and convenient sources first. That's human nature. We should have greeters at our front doors, saying, "Thank you for coming to the best place to find reliable information and good books! How can we help you today?" If we don't offer services, we are just a book warehouse in competition with Amazon.

Google is the new best friend and parent figure for patrons. What's not to like about Google? It's there, it's simple, and it gives you lots of information—way too much information, so patrons look at the first few pages and then give up. Librarians don't do that. If librarians ran the Web, it would be much more organized—perhaps too organized since that has been the basis of our services for generations. That's a great service but not one that patrons recognize since it's behind the scenes. We are the front lines, the reference staff.

Why don't patrons ask for what they need? You can only ask using what you already know. If you don't know what you saw in the sky last night, you can only describe it in terms you know" "bright, reddish, kind of by the moon." If you knew it was Mars, you wouldn't have to ask. If you knew astronomy, you could describe it better. If the librarian knew astronomy, he wouldn't have to look for the information. The difference here is that the librarian knows where to start looking and asking. Was there any noise? Maybe it was a plane. What time did you see it? How high in the sky was it? Was there a meteor shower last night? All those questions can help you narrow the question, even if you don't know any astronomy.

Librarians answer not only what's asked but also what's not asked. Patrons don't know what they don't know; if they did, they would look for it.

Patrons aren't as skilled in information retrieval as we are, or they wouldn't need to ask us. We use lots of jargon, and we can't expect patrons to know our language. The reference interview is the meeting place where we learn each other's languages.

That's not just a figure of speech. We speak our own language, the shortcuts with precise meanings that we all agree on. That's jargon. We speak it; no one else does or cares. Think of that before you use it—if you ever use it with a patron at all. When you struggle to understand that patron who's so shy that he can hardly be heard, the patron with the disability, or the patron who is not a native speaker of your language, think of what you're saying and how. If you're not speaking standard English, how do you expect to come to any understanding at all? The problem may be not the patron's but rather yours.

ASKING THE RIGHT QUESTION

People will very often ask you a question but not what they really want or need to know. That's the hardest part of the reference interview for a new librarian to understand. Why don't they just ask for what they need?

Before the patron asks a librarian, he's usually asked everyone he knows and checked the Web. When he's asking a librarian, it's because he doesn't know what he needs. That's obvious to him since he's already looked everywhere he knows how to. He's asking a librarian as a last resort, the way he goes to the dentist. We think of ourselves as the place to go, but that's often not true. Patrons come to us because we're experts, and people don't expect experts to be friendly and especially helpful but, rather, knowledgeable. They don't look forward to the encounter, so we need to prove ourselves to them.

The patron's first question is often for what he wants. The difference is that what he wants is not always what he needs. It sounds judgmental for us to say that, but the truth is that patrons want information but ask for a book. That's what people associate libraries with: books. He may want a book on boats, but what he needs is a book on building a boat. The patron may not know that there are books on the subject or think that once he gets to the boats section he can find the information he needs. He may not know that there are magazines about boat building or trustworthy websites. He may think that he's making your job easier.

The reality is that they often do ask for what they need. We learn all that jargon in colleges and libraries, but our patrons don't. They tend to ask in plain language, something that some of us have forgotten to use. Our job is to translate their question into a question that we can use to search, something with terms that are useful—for us. Those terms are not useful for patrons outside the library. There's no reason for him to know them: it's our language. The second part of our job is translating our findings into useful information, in plain language, so that the patron's needs are met.

We sometimes forget the second part of our job. We give the patron citations and call numbers and send him on his way. That's like telling the person who's looking for a good restaurant the geographic coordinates for it and telling him to have fun. You wouldn't be satisfied with that; in fact, you're likely to very unhappy with it. You'll never ask that person (or anyone who looks like him) again.

When we don't give the patron the information he needs in a way that he can use easily, we haven't done our job. He doesn't care that you did a terrific search if he can't use the results. If it's not in a language that he understands, it's useless.

Think about it. When was the last time someone called you at home and asked if you'd like to subscribe to a serial? Was that a breakfast serial? Do you give a Boolean operator your call number on the phone? Icon, reserve, fiche, recall, hold—these all have specialized meanings to us and will confuse patrons to no end. Why are we surprised that patrons can confuse us when we speak this strange language of our own?

Think about the doctor-patient model again. You go to the doctor and say your foot hurts and assume he knows what you're talking about. It's pretty simple, right? But he will keep asking. What part of your foot? Toes, heel, top, sole? Does it hurt when you're sitting, standing, walking? All the time or just sometimes? Worse at some one point or doing some particular thing? You finally narrow it down to the sole hurts when you get up in the morning, but it goes away as you walk. You might hear him mutter, "Why didn't you just say that?" He tells you that you have plantar fasciitis, and you look blank. "What's that?" You expect him to explain it and tell you what to do about it. You've just gone through an interview to find out what you need and probably felt a little silly about not just saying that your sole hurt at the beginning, but how do you know how to tell him if you don't know what's important?

That's how patrons feel. They don't have the vocabulary to negotiate the library and find the answer, and your job is to translate. That's why you make the big bucks.

There are exceptions, like directional questions and known item questions, where the patron is asking if you have something and where it is. Those are straightforward and don't require a reference interview. That's why we refer to them as "ready reference," the easy questions that most of our staff can answer. You can check a reference book or database and give the short answer. Those aren't really reference questions and don't require any dialogue. "Down the hall to the left" covers a lot of questions at the desk. It's the other questions where we use our skills and knowledge. Those are the hard ones.

Generally, the patron is not trying to tell you what he knows; he's trying to tell you what he doesn't know. He doesn't have the vocabulary to describe it and may not even be sure that it exists; he simply knows that he needs some information and needs help finding it. That's what makes us professionals: the skill to help him put his need into words and then find what he needs.

Sometimes patrons want to make sure that we're friendly and helpful. That's why they ask one question at first and then ask what they really want to ask. They may ask where the encyclopedias, fiction, or the phone are and decide whether to ask you their real question. If you don't smile and ask if you can be of any other help at that point, they may decide you're not going to be of any real help with the real question.

Their real question may be an important one or an embarrassing one, one that they don't want to reveal to someone who is going to raise their eyebrows and roll their eyes. They want help, not judgment. After all, you may not understand their question and not help at all. This is the point where your people skills will pay off.

MAKING A GOOD FIRST IMPRESSION

The first thing you want to do is look friendly. Smile, make eye contact, and ask how you can help them. Sit up straight or lean toward them a little. That shows interest. Body language is the first thing patrons see, so pay attention to it. Put down anything in your hands. Look up from your monitor. You want to show the patron that he has your undivided attention.

Listen to their question. Really listen and encourage them to elaborate as much as they want. That can be as simple as a nod or "Okay, tell me more." This is active listening, giving the patron some feedback that you're willing to listen to more. Sometimes you get all the information that you need from that first exchange. Once you show interest in them, they will tell you everything you need to know.

If not, keep encouraging them, then ask a few clarifying questions. Ask what format they want or other details—whatever you need to know to get them what they need.

Match your style to the patrons. If the patron uses a low voice, is businesslike, or is a child, you can level the reference interview by adopting their style. Unconsciously, they're telling you something about what they expect from you. Reference desks seldom give the patron any privacy, unlike the offices and consulting rooms of other professionals, so they may be telling you it's personal or just trying to keep your attention amid the ringing phones and the line of waiting patrons.

Taking notes, even a few words, shows that you're taking them seriously, too. The notes may not be of any use to you, as you may have an excellent memory. It's another technique of body language, a nonverbal message.

Don't interrupt them. Don't turn to your computer and start searching or even just open a database that you think you'll use. That's a nonverbal cue from you that the questioning is over, even if that isn't what you mean. You may think you're saving a few seconds, but in reality you may well have to start over again when you have all the facts.

Open questions are the ones that need the patron to give you information, not just a yes or no. Closed questions don't leave any room for elaboration and have only two possible answers: yes or no, this or that. If you offer choices, the patron may choose one of them even if it's not what the patron wants. He may be trying to be pleasant or may think that's all that's available. Open questions leave a lot of room for a real answer. Encourage him to tell you more about what he needs, and keep doing that until you know what it is.

Open questions are also helpful when you don't know much about the subject. "Can you tell me more?" will keep the patron talking about it until you can get the gist of it. If you don't, just say, "I'm not familiar with that. Can you tell me more?" Then you can ask your questions.

THE INTERVIEW ITSELF

How recent does the information need to be? Do you need something from this year, this week, or something updated today? Do you need historical information or background information? This will vary, depending on what the patron will use the information for. You usually want to offer the most recent and up-to-date information, but the patron may need information that's older. For some information, it won't make any difference. The first president of the United States will be George Washington no matter when it was written. Whether he really chopped down the cherry tree will depend on when the source was written.

How much do you need? Do you need everything on an old building or just the date it was built? Do you need a Civil War encyclopedia or a list of the battles, or are you interested in only one? How many sources do you need for a homework assignment? Do you need several books for general background information plus the most recent information? Do you need something short that you can read now? The amount the patron needs will vary according to many factors, including whether the question relates to his job or his hobby.

Do you have a deadline? This is tied into the previous question. You may want everything but have to finish a report tonight. That will narrow the sources. The patron may ask for a series of books but may need a single book that covers the same topics. That's common when he's heard people refer to *Consumer Reports* and doesn't realize that it's not a single book or that the Lord of the Rings is a trilogy and not a single title.

Will you do the research, or will the librarian do it? This ties into the "how-much" question too. Librarians usually have limited time to do research for patrons. If the patron will do the research, does he already have the skills, or will you have to teach him how to use the tools? Will he have to return for instruction later? That varies a great deal between public, academic, and special libraries.

At what level does the information need to be? A popular book on cats or a veterinary text? Something for beach reading or something for a long winter's night? Something for your toddler daughter or for your mother? Information that's too technical for a toddler or too simple for a professional will not be useful for either.

How much detail do you need? Will a book on old Fords work, or do you need a manual on repairing a specific model? Too much information is just as bad in reference as it is in a social situation, but too little isn't going to be helpful either.

Where did you hear about this? This is helpful when the patron is vague about the information. If the patron heard about it on a TV show or read it in a magazine, you will have an easier time tracking it down or at least what he heard where. Finding the actual information can be trickier if it isn't in print, but you can always offer the contact information for the show or station. In a perfect world, you'll make the call too. In the real world, some of these questions come after businesses are closed, the station staff have gone home, or the magazine is sold out.

What format would you like the information in? Do you want *The Lion King*— the movie, the musical, the book, the score, or the CD? There are often several forms of the same information or article. If it's in a database, you may be able to e-mail it directly to him. If it's a book, you may have it on CD or in large print. Perhaps a graph or map that makes the information visually accessible is the best. Offer the patron all the choices that are available

How are you going to be using it? A speech to a business group or a homework assignment? A presentation to a Boy Scout board or a project for Boy Scouts? That will make a difference in the amount and format the patron needs. The answer might rule out some sources or point you to the best one for him.

Some patrons will see those questions as prying, so it helps to add, "Knowing that would help me find something appropriate." It's important to use "how you will use it" instead of "why you need it." You want to keep a neutral and professional interest and not imply a personal one. Some patrons still won't give you more information, so you will have to work with what you have. Keep using your encouraging skills, and hopefully they will correct you if you get off course. Some patrons will refuse to answer other questions until you establish trust again.

Some questions you can try are the following:

"Can you tell me a little about how you're going to use the information? That will help me find the right thing for you."
"Can you tell me how the question came up? That may help me find an answer."
"Can you tell me a little about the background? Some context may help us find the answer."

Repeat and rephrase the question to be sure you really do understand. Remember the breakfast serial? Maybe you misheard and need to start again. Perhaps the patron works in a field that has its own jargon and you don't understand it. Keep clarifying until you agree on what the goal is. Paraphrasing lets the patron hear their question again and to add to it or clarify it. Every time you change the question, rephrase it until you both know exactly what you're talking about.

Verify spellings routinely. It may be a simple word or name, but you may have heard it wrong. Does the patron swim weekly or weakly? You can save both of you time by confirming the spelling. If you get it wrong, own the mistake. "I'm afraid I misheard you" or "Sorry, my mistake" aren't that hard to say once you get used to them—but you can avoid them by verifying. Verifying is especially important when you are taking notes to refer a question or research it later. You may remember how the name is pronounced now but not tomorrow. The librarian you refer the question to will not have a clue unless you have it in your notes.

LOOKING FOR THE ANSWER

The correct answer is the one that's most useful for this patron. A four-year-old boy once asked his grandfather, "Why are there trees?" He answered in great detail how trees exchange oxygen for carbon dioxide in the atmosphere, how the biomass decomposes and returns nutrients to the soil, how they create shade, and how they conserve water. He walked away, and his mother asked him if Grandpa answered the question. He shrugged and said, "I just wanted to know if they were there to hold birds up!" It was a correct answer but the wrong one for the questioner. That's a common mistake. Be sure your answer is to the patron's real question and not the one that gets asked most often or an answer you already know.

Sometimes what patrons want doesn't exist: Google's business plan for next 50 years, Lincoln's baby pictures, or the original Bible. You can refer them somewhere else, but the ethical thing is to be honest and say that they don't exist. You can ask if there's another way to fill their need—Google's website, early photos of Lincoln, or very old Bibles—but if you've done your research and they don't exist, you can save the patron's time with honesty. That doesn't mean that he won't come back and ask another librarian in an hour, though. If you see the patron coming back frequently, it's a good time to file your findings in your wiki.

Finding the real question is just the first part of the reference interview. If you stop here, you may give the patron the right information but not in a form he can use or a language he understands. Now that you know what he wants, find out how he wants it.

How much information does he need? Remember the question about trees? Your patron may just need an answer or may need two articles for an assignment or may be working on his thesis and need everything you have on the subject. Implied in the "how-much" question is "how much are you willing to do?" Is the patron willing to read several books or many articles? Does he have time to?

Some questions will not have a single definitive answer and may have several sources. Is global warming real? Does evil exist? Tell your patron what resources exist and ask him if he's looking for a particular finding or an overview the issue. Let him make the determination of what he needs at this point. He may be a debater who needs one side for his arguments or a student who needs all sides of what he thought was a simple issue.

Returning to the retail model, you are a personal shopper for information. Some patrons are hunters who want to get their information and leave. Some are gatherers who want to look at everything and then decide what they want.

Your job is to match the patron with what he needs in the form he needs or wants. You're the matchmaker, but your job doesn't include a shotgun wedding. It's not your job to tell the patron what he needs; rather, it's your job to give him his options and let him decide. After all, you will invite him back to shop again if it doesn't fit his needs.

There are sources that aren't in your library, too. Archives, museums, and government offices all have information that isn't published and not available in print or online. Often it's great information, but the patron will have to go or call them when they're open. Some patrons aren't willing to travel or don't have time to. You can always give them the contact information or make a referral, but often they will settle for what you have at hand. Remember, good enough is good enough for most people, but they will have the contact information if they change their minds later.

Asking the patron what he has found so far isn't a test; it's an acknowledgment that he has been working on finding information on his own. If he hasn't started yet, you can suggest a starting place, and he hasn't lost any face. The key is to phrase it so that it doesn't sound like a reprimand or a challenge.

"What have you found already? I don't want to repeat your work" acknowledges that the patron has already started working on his question. It also establishes that he is in control and that you are working at his direction. Many librarians will bristle at that suggestion, but that's what patron service is: if you're not looking for what he needs, you're not helping him at all. There are many other tasks that librarians do, but patrons don't really care about whether you have published or have the next day's children's programming ready or the new books cataloged. Those are behind-the-scene tasks, and reference means that you are on the front lines.

Think of the so-called big-box store. If a stock person ignores you while you look for canned beans, you will ignore him and perhaps not return to that store. If he asks you what kind of beans you want and your favorite brand and then walks you to them, you'll have good memories and feelings about the store and come back. Retail stores have studied how to serve patrons, and you can learn a lot from the good ones. The analogy is that it doesn't matter how many books or online resources you have if you don't help people find and use them and do so graciously.

Helping a patron identify search terms helps him go from asking questions to finding answers. You can model how to start with a broad search and narrow it down to a useful one. World War II is a huge subject. What, in particular, is he interested in? Not the battles as much as the home front. A certain part? What people did for fun. Now you have a topic in a size that's usable for searching and the patron's real interest: recreational activities during World War II. If that proves too broad, you can help him narrow it again. Women, men, or children? At home, alone, or in groups?

The opposite is also possible. A subject can be too narrow to find a source. Embroidery needles between the years 1400 and 1450 won't turn much up, but widening the search to sewing in the Middle Ages will turn up images and research on sewing at that time.

MODELING HOW TO SEARCH

Showing the patron how you use resources models how he can use them. He may or may not remember what you show him, but it is part of your job, too. Remember that patrons are people, not just patrons. They have lives outside the library, they have other problems to worry about, and they may not remember a word that you said or a thing that you showed, but they will remember that you were helpful. That's a valuable takeaway for the library. Another old adage from retail is that a happy customer will tell a friend and that an unhappy one will tell 10 friends. Good word of mouth is one of your most valuable assets in a library.

Let your patron watch you search and tell him what you're doing. That accomplishes several things. It lets the patron know you're working on his question, it gives him a chance to correct you if he sees a mistake, and it lets him follow along and see what you're doing and why. It also gives the patron another chance to refine or redirect the search. If you can, turn your monitor so that he can see the screen and follow you. If you use new search terms or a new database, write them down or print them out so he can replicate your search on his own.

Keep letting the patron give you feedback, and if he doesn't, ask for it. "Are we getting warm here?" gives him a chance to correct your path or, if he's still uncertain of what he's looking for, to keep looking.

Don't stop looking if the answer isn't where you expect it to be. That's especially true of subscription databases, where the mix of journals may change monthly. Keep your patron apprised of what you're doing: "I thought that journal was in Ebsco, but let me check it in another database. It'll just take a moment." Widen your search when you need to. If the patron is asking for an article on the treatment of alcoholism, your first thought may be a social work database, but there may be many in Cinahl. Think of synonyms while you search. "Treatment," "medical," "nursing," "social work," "alcoholism," and "addiction" are all terms that might work, even if the patron didn't suggest them. That's why he came to you for help. You know how to create key words on the fly, and you know how to find search terms in the online public access catalog.

Should you use Google and other search engines? Sure, why not? If you're looking for an online source, certainly use them. Use your bookmarks and pathfinders. If you're looking for a book, especially one you don't have in your library, try Google Books. Not all books are there, but you can do a quick check and make sure that you have the right *Spot the Dog* or the right edition of *Tom Sawyer* in mind. If you only have a partial citation for a book, this can be a fast check. If it's a title that is in the public domain (before 1923), you can try Project Gutenberg to check it or one of the many open-source book sources.

It also gives you a chance to show the patron how to use search engines well. Most people search with the first terms they started with; you may know better terms and sites that will give patrons vetted sources. Many people know how to "Google" but not how to do it well and are disappointed with the results they get. You should know how to do it well. Google and other search engines have help pages and tips that you should know and keep up with.

If you only have a partial or an incorrect citation for an article, try Google Scholar. A search with a partial or incorrect title or author will usually turn up the correct one. If not, you've lost only a few seconds looking. Google Scholar will also tell you the places where it can be found. That may include databases, print, the Web, institutional repositories, and archives. Institutional repositories, where faculty and students can archive papers that have been submitted for publication, are a good source for academic papers.

The ability to remember where to look is probably better than an encyclopedic memory. Albert Einstein is reputed to have said, "Why should I memorize anything I can look up in a book?" He would have been a fan of Google and databases. You can start a wiki for the reference staff or a frequently-asked-questions site for patrons and have a notebook to jot things down until you get them online. You should share what you've found with other members of your staff unless you work alone. In that case, there's no one to remind you, and you should keep notes anyway.

Don't be afraid of ambiguity, referring people to other librarians, or looking silly. Have a sense of humor about yourself and your mistakes, as everyone makes them. Laughter destresses, humanizes, and relaxes. You want to project a professional attitude, but professional doesn't mean stuffy, and making mistakes just means you're human, too. How you handle mistakes is what makes you a professional. Acknowledge them and go on.

INVITING THE PATRON BACK AGAIN

Now that you've found the answer, remember that you're not done yet. You want to invite patrons back if that's not the information they need or if they need more help. Patrons sometimes feel that they've "used up their quota" after talking to a librarian, and it would be pushy to come back and ask another question. If you have a chance to take them to the resource or show them how to use it, do so. If you see them later, ask them if the resource you recommended worked for them. Following up is an important part of the reference transaction. Ask the patron if you've answered his question and answered it completely. You may have, and he may have thought of something else to ask you. Smile and start again. Remember, you don't have a limit on how many questions you can answer. Your goal is to get the information to the patron.

Again, like in retail, you don't want the patron leaving empty-handed. Patrons often don't know about interlibrary loan or realize that you have databases that aren't part of the Web they search at home. You may have microforms and magazines. Patrons may not realize that what's on the shelves is just a fraction of what you have access to. It's your job to tell them about the information they can't see. If the source isn't in your library, give your patron all the options he has. It may be that the only option is to call an agency himself or travel to a distant archive. Make sure he has the information to take with him: an address, a phone number, a name, or whatever you can provide to get him to the information.

Now that you know how to conduct the reference interview, be prepared to do it over and over and with multiple patrons. That's the juggling act you may face at busy times. You can interview patron A and get him started looking at sources, then give patron B his directions to the videos, and then interview patron C and get him started while you check back with patron A. You may have to add phone calls and e-mails to the mix.

That's why you want to have priorities established before you face this situation. Who gets helped next, and who can you delay? Can you answer the phone and get the patron's number so that you can call him back later? Can you ask who has a directional question and answer it before taking the next person in line? Can you call on someone to help? You need to know what your options are before you get into a situation that adds to your stress. You also need to explain what you're doing to the patrons and assure them that you will be only a minute and then you can give him all your attention. If you don't, it's as rude as turning your back on him.

HELPING WITH SELF-SERVICE

Both patrons and librarians use what they know and are familiar with, even if it's not the best source or it's outdated. Patrons often use what agrees with what they already think; they want to support their views. You need to stay current with new sources and know where to look for them. You need to introduce these sources to patrons, either in person or by a display or "new!" tag. When patrons don't ask you questions, that doesn't mean they don't have any; they're just not asking you. You can make their lives simpler by making sure that things on your shelves are labeled clearly and that displays are fresh and current. You can't lead a horse to water or make him drink, but you can make it obvious and attractive enough that your patron finds it on his own.

Patrons will use Wikipedia. Why not? It's not the best source, but it's there, and it's easy to use. Teach your patrons that it's a good place to start, like an encyclopedia, but not always correct or complete. Following the footnotes is a good path to follow. They will lead to print and online sources, which will lead to others.

Patrons, especially students, are pretty good at using Google. They are rarely good at framing search terms or limiting their results. They are rarely good at analyzing and synthesizing the results. You can offer to help but don't be surprised if they refuse. If you make it apparent that you are willing to help, they will come to you when they need it.

Students sometimes think that information is cut and dried—or cut and paste in the case of papers due. One source is as good as another, information is information, and if it's online, it must be true. Finding good information is often a new idea, and using the information to create new information is even newer. Students are students after all; if they knew, they wouldn't be asking you for help. You should reward them for asking you and not their Facebook friends. It's not your job to do their homework, but you can show them how to evaluate information and how to locate good sources.

Patrons and librarians will use Google. It's simply too easy and ubiquitous not to. Google is the ready-reference source for our generation. Google has some great features for librarians, though. Google can find incomplete citations better than paper indexes. It's good for incorrect citations since you can check spelling by the results and suggestions offered. That's especially good for names. It's also good for tip-of-the-tongue questions, the ones where the patron *almost* knows the name. Google Sets will let you list related terms and suggest missing ones (Cirasella 2007).

Many libraries now use tiered reference, where a paraprofessional answers directional and ready-reference questions and refers more complicated ones to the librarian. It's important that staff identify themselves as nonlibrarians for difficult questions so that the patron knows he'll get better service from the referral and isn't just being brushed off. It may be hard for the staff to say they need help when they may be perfectly able to help the patron with his initial question. If you have a tiered system, work with your staff on finding good ways to refer patrons when they need more help. You might want to refer to the medical model again—the nurse is perfectly competent to give you a shot or diagnose a sore throat but not more complicated diagnoses and procedures. Defining that cutoff point is the hard part, and you need to justify it with more than "I'm the professional here." You may have to rethink your roles and duties. After all, the idea of tiered reference is to give the patron good service and to free the librarian for professional duties; you'll have to define your role as well as the staff role.

How confusing is your library? Do you get lots of directional questions that take your time? They may be feelers to see if you're friendly, but it may not. Send someone out with a video camera to get a patron's-eye view of your signage. You may know where the northwest corner is, but who carries a compass with them? Directional questions are not bad things per se, but most adults don't want to have to ask to find a restroom.

MANAGING YOUR TIME TO SAVE TIME

Time can be a problem in reference interviews. You have a line of people waiting for help (hopefully), and they have other places to go and things to do. You can tell the people in line that you will be with them shortly. You can see if anyone has a simple question, like a directional one that can be answered in a sentence. Don't just ask them, though; tell the patron you're working with what you are doing. "Do you mind if I ask if he has a quick question?" tells the first patron that you'll be back with him shortly and acknowledges the second.

You can prioritize your patrons, and you should. Do you help patrons who are physically there before answering the phone? Do you help patrons in the order they come? Is returning a call to a patron more important than answering an e-mail? Those things may vary over the course of a day, too. How long should a patron wait before he is helped? Can you call someone on backup duty or get their question and call them later?

Working at a desk is like juggling. You have to keep an eye on all the things you have going on. You can get a patron started on something, answer a ready-reference question, have someone hold while you check a source, and then answer it and go to your first patron to see if he needs more help. That's one of the reasons for inviting the patron back if he doesn't find what he needs. Sometimes we forget. We shouldn't, and that's an important part of the interview. You can keep quick notes on who you have to follow up with. "Plaid jacket, cars" on your list will remind you of who and what.

If a patron has a complicated question and doesn't need an immediate answer, schedule a consultation where you can spend more uninterrupted time. Many patrons will appreciate the chance to have your undivided attention, and you can work without worrying about the next patron. Consultations are also a good suggestion when the patron is uncomfortable asking the question. It gives him a little privacy and time for you to gain his trust.

People who have deadlines—students, businesspeople, or people with young children—need information fast. Students, especially, are in the library because they need to be there—to write a paper or to do research—not because they want to be there. They see the library like a dentist's office: they go because they need to go, not always willingly. Students expect everything to be available online and free and, most of all, quick. "Waiting for an interlibrary loan" is not in their vocabulary until a few years into college.

A "sufficient" answer for simple questions can likely be found online. Some people, especially students, want "good enough." There's no real goal or interest except the grade. They are human, after all, and who does more work than is necessary for the job? In the real world, we call that "efficiency." There are different levels of "good enough," too. Good enough for a two-page paper is not good enough for a 10-page one, and an illustration good enough for a library orientation paper to prove you've been in the library isn't good enough for a thesis. Good enough for a high school student isn't good enough for a genealogist.

More and more, the key question of the reference interview is not "What do you need?" but "How do you need it delivered?" Going to the library and getting a book is no longer the gold standard. Information can be delivered in many forms and via many media, and by the time you read this, probably a dozen more will exist. To the patron, the delivery method may be as important as the information itself. For a patron with a disability or a distance learner, the media may determine what's usable.

ROVING REFERENCE

We say we want to be at the user's point of need, and in the physical library, we can do that literally. With an inexpensive netbook or a cell phone, you can check the catalog, consult an expert, and e-mail a Web page to the patron. Yes, you may feel like a Wal-Mart greeter, but what's wrong with someone greeting you at the door and asking if they can help? It seems to work in retail, it works in offices, and it works in general. There's no longer any reason to be anchored to a desk or even a library.

But, you say, you're a professional with a master's degree. Your ministers or priests have doctorates, they still greet people and mingle, and no one thinks they're unprofessional. Librarians are more than a little sensitive about being regarded as professionals, but we need to get over it. Is it all that bad to be thought of as a good, intelligent, helpful person rather than as a professional?

Remember, the reference interview is an interview, and it works as well as or better than a man-in-the-street one as a behind-a-desk one. You're a professional because of what you know, not where you are.

If you're in the stacks and don't look lost, someone will ask you a question. Shelvers get more questions than librarians in many cases. Why? Because they're there, right now, and obviously work at the library. Without a desk between you and without a line of people waiting (if you're lucky), anyone becomes more approachable. That's one of the reasons people rely on family and friends for information.

You might want to wear something more obvious than a name tag. Lots of people have name tags, and lots of people come in the library after work wearing them. Nothing is quite as embarrassing as asking a doctor for help in a grocery store. A shirt with the library logo, a bright vest, or a silly hat with an "Ask Me, I Know" button will identify you as a person to ask. In a small library, you may be a familiar face, but in a large one, you're just another face in the crowd. You're offering a service, and you need to advertise it.

Many people have cell phones. They use them in the library no matter how may signs you put up. Do you have signs with the reference phone number? Does your staff have your number on their quick-dial list so that they can get an answer from you when they encounter a patron? How about putting your phone number in the stacks so that patrons can call and ask and you can meet them in the stacks or at their work stations? You can literally meet them at their point of need.

When people see you answering a question or helping someone else, it encourages them to ask since you're obviously knowledgeable and helpful. They may not even need to ask if they're listening to you and you answered the question. Roving also gives you the advantage of talking to people while you take them where the information is, saving time for both of you.

Have an "I'll be back, I'm helping someone" sign that you can leave at the desk while you're gone. That tells patrons not only that you'll be back but also that you're helpful. If you're at the desk and can't leave, maybe a student assistant or staff member can take them to find a known item.

Roving can be outside your building, too. You can have a "home" in an academic department, a bookmobile, a retirement home, or a community center. With netbooks and cell phones, you can be contacted by patrons wherever you are and refer a patron to where he needs to be. Pennsylvania State University outfitted a hot dog cart with a sign and a laptop that can be wheeled around the campus. That's not just good marketing, it's service to go.

To answer questions, though, you need to have access to information. If you have access to databases and reliable websites, you're all set. Be prepared for referring people to the library and the frowns that will greet you. You can temper that by putting a book on hold for the patron, ordering by interlibrary loan online, or referring him to a subject specialist or another repository. It's a good teachable moment: just like librarians aren't just at the reference desk, information isn't just at the library or just in books, but some information is and will be for some time to come.

If you are a liaison to another facility or an academic department, you can conduct the interview in advance of the need. At an office, in a meeting, or over coffee, you can ask the patron about plans for upcoming projects and have everything in place when it's needed. You can offer reading lists, bibliographies, tours, and referrals that will meet his needs. You can have regular meetings or advertise where you will be and when.

IN SEARCH OF THE GOOD BOOK: READERS' ADVISORY

Unlike the factual question, readers' advisory questions aren't about information; they're about pleasure. People read for enjoyment, for adventure, for inspiration, to learn about people just like them, and to learn about people who are nothing like them. This is true not only of fiction, although fiction is the largest part of reading for pleasure. Nonfiction can be just as exciting, spiritual, or interesting as fiction, except it's true. Truth does limit the possibilities of a story, but there are hybrids that mix both without those limitations.

The great difference between reading for facts and reading for fun is what the patron wants from the experience. The researcher wants information, whereas the reader wants an experience. He doesn't want to learn something but wants to feel something. He wants to connect to something or someone. The hard part is matching that reader with the book he will connect with.

That book will be different for each reader. John may love *Moby Dick* and the whaling background, the isolation of the crew, the "quest" plot, and the absence of women. James may think it's the worst book in the world: too long and too detailed, with nothing happening until the end of the book. Jane may think it's the *Lord of the Flies* at sea. Jodie thinks it would make a great anchor for his boat. They're all correct because reading for pleasure is about enjoying the book. If the patron doesn't enjoy it, it's not a good book—for him.

Never recommend a book just because it's a classic, either in literature or simply in its genre. It may be a terrific book for generations of readers and may have wowed the critics, but you're working with this single reader, and it's your job to get him a book he'll enjoy. Don't try to change his tastes, as they are his tastes. The idea that a librarian's job is to "better" his patrons has no place in a readers' advisory—if it has any place in the modern library at all.

Patrons may enjoy books that teach them something in their context, like a novel about a horse trainer. You can ask if it's the horses they liked or animals in general—maybe they would like James Herriott's books. Maybe it was the western setting, or maybe it was in Kentucky—don't make assumptions about books you don't know. Perhaps it's the time period, the manners, or the social structure—or maybe it's none of that.

You can also ask what movies a patron likes. Some are based on books and short stories, and many are based on popular genres. If a patron liked *Blade Runner*, he might like Philip K. Dick's "Do Androids Dream of Electric Sheep?," the story it's based on, or other stories by him. That's not a given, though; maybe it was the special effects he liked.

The important things to the readers' advisory is to ask what the patron likes and why and to give the reader a choice of books. Never suggest that you have the "right" book; just give good suggestions. Offer a selection and let him choose what he wants. You can say that people have said good things about this one or that they liked the characters in that one and let him make up his own mind.

Never recommend a book based on what you like. It's not bad that you like it, but the reader didn't ask what you like. In advisories, all opinions are equal, so what you like is no more relevant than what his brother or grocer likes.

Talk about the nonplot factors of the book rather than the plot. "Warm," "romantic," "cheerful," "scary," "suspenseful," and "serious" are just a few of the adjectives for mood. What about characters? Struggling single parent, gay teen, fatherly detective, or hard-boiled teacher? How about the setting? Victorian England, medieval Italy, or South American politics? More action than description? These are all things that you can garner from book jackets or reviews without reading the book.

Best sellers and Oprah's List books are sure winners. That creates a problem when you don't have enough copies for every reader. There are always wait lists, but it's good to have read-alikes ready or to have previous books by the author. Read the reviews and find similar themes and authors so that you can offer something to the patron while he waits. Having read-alike lists and displays makes it easier to make suggestions.

Some publishers make it easy to find similar genre books. Romances may have similar covers or titles; the "Love's Adjective Noun" series springs to mind. All by different authors, all had titles like "Love's Passionate Fury" and "Love's Seething Passion." The police procedurals may have badges prominently featured on the covers, or the family sagas will feature a group portrait. What works for the bookstores works for the library as well. They also create instant coordinated displays.

If a patron asks if you've read a book, just smile and say that the library has too many to read or that you haven't had time for that one but you've heard good things about it. That's a pretty safe statement; that is, someone in the library chose it because they thought it had value. Don't make value judgments about genres or books you don't like. Practice comments that don't make you a liar. "These are very popular romances" can cover formulaic paperbacks. "I've heard good things form other patrons about this," "This got good reviews," and "He's got a real following" are value-free statements that you can use without giving your opinion of a book (Saricks 2005).

Sometimes patrons will ask you for "a nice story." That may be code for "no violence, no divorce, no drama, and certainly no sex!" Don't be judgmental, as the patron may be going through a divorce that includes family violence and wants to get away from the subject. The patron may be looking for his grand-mother, who doesn't like sex and violence. The "nice story" includes some very good books that just don't happen to have anything objectionable. This is another good topic for a list.

Patrons look for things besides facts. Many are looking for something to read—and not just "something" but an entertaining book in a genre they like and a topic that interests them. Don't send the patron to the online public access cata-log, and don't go there yourself. You know—and the patron knows—that the online public access catalog isn't going to tell you if it's a good read. Neither is Amazon.com, as its "alikes" are based on sales, not themes or styles.

TOOLS FOR READERS

Show patrons how to use readers' advisory tools and let them watch you use them. Does the patron want to learn from the book or feel something after read-ing it? What reading skills does it require? What physical characteristics does it need to have: being large print, lightweight, or purse sized?

You can help in advance by making it easy for the patron. Sort books as your patrons like them: as good reads, read-alikes, or genre. You can do it passively. You can use spine labels, have displays, have handouts and new arrivals lists, online or on paper, and in several languages.

You'll ask different questions for the advisory. Ask the patron to tell you about a book he liked or about an author or a series. What did he like about it: the plot, the characters (male or female or young or old), the theme (family, friendship, good versus evil, or revenge), the pace, the setting, the period, the ending, the length, or the mood? (Sheldrick et al. 2002, p. 162). There are many subgenres, too. Science fiction has futurist, fantasy, sword and sorcery, and many others. There are high-interest/low-skill books, which are good for low-level readers, vacation reads, and teens. Tweens, teens, and young adults have their own genres that include things like vampire romances. You can't read them all; this is a field where you can rely on advice from others. If a patron wants a genre you don't know, there are plenty of tools you can look into.

Make a point of reading a book or two in each genre. You may struggle with a genre that you don't like, but make it through the first chapter or two. That's where the "hook" is—the plot point, feeling, or action that draws you into the story. That will give you some insight into the genre or author. You may find that you like it more than you thought you would. There's a reason why people buy and read them after all.

For recreational reading, people want something different than the factual information you find in reference questions. They are looking for a mood, a feeling, an adventure, or either something that they can't do physically themselves, like piracy, or something they want to feel but don't. That's different for each reader. Some read *Harry Potter* because they like fantasy, some because it has strong female characters, some because a boy overcomes his past, some for the adventure, and some for romance. Many books have something for everyone or at least many people.

This is a great place for a wiki, especially one where your readers can contribute. Divide it by categories or themes or anything your readers want to. Anyone can add to it, and anyone can correct it. If that's too unstructured for your library, try a blog. You can have approval privileges on the posts that way and prevent spam, but it will require someone to monitor it. You can have staff write reviews of what they've read and post them. You can open it up for your patrons. You can use one for your book clubs. You can tweet about new novels. You can post them to Facebook. Repurposing those posts from one medium to another will save you time, and more people will see them. It doesn't take long to copy and paste, and it's never a bad thing to have publicity. You can do the same for frequent reference questions, too.

Advisories are fertile ground for visual representation, where you can choose a book like you order coffee: a touch of Turow, a dash of Grisham, a little Martini on the side, lots of action, but no sex. You can find read-alikes by characteristics without having to consult a list or find the mood you're looking for and a book to fit it. Some databases already offer visualization to patrons for refining questions. There are a number of open-source programs that use it, or you can use the tag cloud created by a blog. The important part is that it's interactive, and the patron not only can use it but also can contribute to it. It makes the patron one of your allies and takes still another task off your list.

REFERENCES

Cirasella, Jill. "You and Me and Google Makes Three: Welcoming Google into the Reference Interview." *Library Philosophy and Practice* (2007). http://www.webpages.uidaho.edu/~mbolin/cirasella.htm (accessed September 24, 2010).

Radcliff, Carolyn J. "Interpersonal Communication with Library Patrons: Physician-Patient Research Models." *RQ* 34, no. 4 (Summer 1995): 497–506.

Ranganathan, S. R. *The Five Laws of Library Science*. Madras: Madras Library Association, 1931.

Saricks, Joyce G. *Readers' Advisory Service in the Public Library*. Chicago: American Library Association, 2005.

Sheldrick Ross, Catherine et al. *Conducting the Reference Interview: A How-To-Do-It Manual for Librarians*. New York: Neal-Schuman, 2002.

FURTHER READING

Beard, David, and Kate Vo Thi-Beard. "Rethinking the Book: New Theories for Readers' Advisory." *Reference & User Services Quarterly* 47, no. 4 (Summer 2008): 331–35.

Becker, C. "Student Values and Research: Are Millennials Really Changing the Future of Reference and Research?" *Journal of Library Administration* 49, no. 4 (May 2009): 341–64.

Bopp, Richard E., and Linda C. Smith. *Reference and Information Services: An Introduction.* 3rd ed. Westport, CT: Libraries Unlimited, 2001.

Carlile, Heather. "The Implications of Library Anxiety for Academic Reference Services: A Review of the Literature." *Australian Academic & Research Libraries* 38, no. 2 (June 2007): 129–47.

Dewdney, P., and G. Michell. "Asking 'Why' Questions in the Reference Interview: A Theoretical Justification." *Library Quarterly* 67, no. 1 (1997): 50–71.

Ford, Charlotte. *Crash Course in Reference.* Westport, CT: Libraries Unlimited, 2008.

Green, Samuel S. "Personal Relations between Librarians and Readers." *Library Journal* 1, no. 2/3 (1876): 74–81.

Herald, Diana Tixier. *Genreflecting: A Guide to Popular Reading Interests.* 6th ed. Westport, CT: Libraries Unlimited, 2006. Part of a popular series of readers advisory guides for genres and ages.

Jennerich, Zaremba, and Edward J. Jennerich. *The Reference Interview as a Creative Art.* 2nd ed. Westport, CT: Libraries Unlimited, 1997.

Lorenzen, Michael. "Management by Wandering Around: Reference Rovering and Quality Reference Services." *The Reference Librarian* 28, no. 59 (1997): 51–57.

Maatta, Stephanie L. *A Few Good Books: Using Contemporary Readers' Advisory Strategies to Connect Readers with Books.* New York: Neal-Schuman, 2010.

Mabry, C. H. "The Reference Interview as Partnership: An Examination of Librarian, Library User, and Social Interaction." *The Reference Librarian* 83–84 (2003): 41–56.

Mills, J. and D. Lodge. "Affect, Emotional Intelligence and Librarian-User Interaction." *Library Review* 55, no. 9 (2006): 587–97.

Pearl, Nancy. *BOOK LUST: Recommended Reading for Every Mood, Moment, and Reason.* Seattle: Sasquatch Books, 2003.

Radford, Marie. *The Reference Encounter: Interpersonal Communication in the Academic Library.* Chicago: American Library Association, 1998.

Robinson, William C. "The Reference Interview." http://web.utk.edu/~wrobinso/590ref_interview.html (accessed September 23, 2010).

Ross, Catherine Sheldrick. "The Reference Interview: Why It Needs to Be Used in Every (Well, Almost Every) Reference Transaction." *Reference & User Services Quarterly* 43, no. 1 (September 22, 2003): 38–42.

Ross, Catherine Sheldrick, Kirsti Nilsen, and Marie L. Radford. *Conducting the Reference Interview: A How-to-Do-It Manual for Librarians.* 2nd ed. New York: Neal-Schuman, 2009.

Ryan, S. "Reference Transactions Analysis: The Cost-Effectiveness of Staffing a Traditional Academic Reference Desk." *Journal of Academic Librarianship* 34, no. 5 (2008): 389–99.

Saxton, Matthew Locke, and John V. Richardson. "Bibliography for Understanding Reference Transactions: Transforming an Art into a Science." http://polaris.gseis.ucla.edu/jrichardson/dis220/urt.htm (accessed September 13, 2010). Contains 1,000 entries on the reference interview.

Stover, Kaite Mediatore. "Stalking the Wild Appeal Factor: Readers' Advisory and Social Networking Sites." *Reference & User Services Quarterly* 48, no. 3 (Spring 2009): 243–44, 245–46, 269.

Taylor, Robert S. "Question-Negotiation and Information Seeking in Libraries." *College and Research Libraries* 29 (1968): 178–94.

Thomsen, Elizabeth. *Rethinking Reference: The Reference Librarian's Practical Guide for Surviving Constant Change*. New York: Neal-Schuman, 1999.

Tyckoson, David A. "Reference at Its Core: The Reference Interview." *Reference & User Services Quarterly* 43, no. 1 (Fall 2003): 49–51.

Wyatt, Neal. *The Readers' Advisory Guide to Nonfiction*. Chicago: American Library Association, 2007.

2 SPECIAL PATRONS AND QUESTIONS

All of your patrons are special and unique. Some will have particular needs and abilities, though that require a different style on your part. They may range from shy children to rowdy adults, but you'll have to deal with them all. There are skills you need to know at the reference desk and beyond since you are the one actually out in the library dealing with the patrons.

You will use all the questions you use in the usual reference interview but need to adapt them to this group of patrons. You'll also learn more skills that you can use in the more usual interview. You can never have too many tricks and tips in your interview bag. They all come in handy.

CHILDREN

Few libraries are made for kids. The online catalog is way too difficult for many adults, let alone children, to use. Library of Congress classification subjects don't include the terms that children use. The Dewey Decimal System is not much easier. Catalogs are written at a much higher reading level than most children have. None are written to answer the question "What kind of kitty do I have?" You will need the reference interview with most children since their vocabularies may not match their curiosity.

Children may not realize that they can ask librarians questions. They are taught not to talk to strangers, not to question adults, and to be quiet. Those lessons may not take, but those are the ideals that they hear. You will need to be more welcoming of children than you may think since some children are shy as well. Roving, moving through the department, and asking if you can help a patron instead of waiting for him to come to your desk is even more effective when working with younger patrons.

Reference for children is just like for adults, but it's also different. Children are even less clear about what they want and less patient. You need to be the one with the patience. It helps to break the interview into short steps that the child can remember and use, then return to you for more help. Take the interview in short steps and provide lots of encouragement and praise. You may rephrase a question and get a totally different response, as the child's mind may be on something else altogether. Young children are not linear thinkers, and you may have a hard time keeping up with them.

Children don't have any experience with jargon, search terms, or giving details. You'll need to clarify often and keep the patron focused on the question at hand. If the child can't spell the word, ask about its context. Did they hear it in science class or in *Avatar*, on *Sesame Street*, or on *Nature?* That can give you a clue.

Although children have a sense of humor and play, try to keep your attitude professional. If you don't, you'll end up playing 20 Questions or guessing if they're serious or joking. Children love to play jokes on adults, and librarians aren't immune.

Don't ask leading questions. Children will tell you what they think you want to hear. They get a lot of experience with that and are dependent on pleasing adults for most of their needs. Use open-ended questions with lots of encouragement.

You always want to check spellings when working with children. Distinguishing between "the Viking War" and "what Vikings wore" is all the harder when the patron is missing his two front teeth. Clarify the question, too. New York: the state or the city? A seven-year-old in Kansas may not know they're not the same or that West Virginia isn't just the left part on the state map. Don't assume that children have the "common knowledge" that adults have.

Don't assume that children know the rules for the library, either. Rules are different between school and public libraries and different still from bookstores. To a child, all these may be just "places with books." You may have to read the rules to children and to some children several times. Bookmarks and posters with simple versions of the rules and some of the international symbols mean that children can take these with them and get familiar with them. Choose your rules carefully. Concentrate on the behavioral ones, like no eating and no running. Younger children will not understand or even need to know what your overdue fines are or the circulation period is. You can tell the parent that. For older children, a handout or bookmark can be more detailed.

Much of a child's library use will center on homework. It's a good practice to have contacts with your local schools before school starts, be that with teachers, boards, or the state level. Some teachers give the same assignments year after year; ask for a copy of them. Some have new ideas every year; it's helpful to know in advance so that you can order materials that will help students. Most areas have their curriculum online or available from the Board of Education. You can find out what grade they will study a subject in and order books or prepare reading lists.

When you do know when the subject will be studied, a display or list can let the children pick their own materials. That lets them choose something that's at the appropriate reading level no matter what their grade level is. Have some videos and picture books, too. Be sure to include encyclopedias in your lists, as children sometimes think that books that look the same are the same and don't think of looking in another volume.

Children assume that information is in one of three places: with family and friends, online, or in books. If they don't ask for an article and it seems appropriate, introduce them to journals and explain how they differ from popular magazines. You'll probably need to do that with tweens and teens, too.

Do you remember when summer vacation seemed years away and then seemed to last only a week? Children have a different sense of time and have a hard time planning ahead. When you ask if they found what they need, ask if they know what they'll need next. Don't assume that all questions are school questions, but school is a child's work, so treat them as real and important.

Make questions a win-win situation. If the child has already looked for information, congratulate him. If he hasn't, congratulate him on the decision to ask a librarian. Look at all the time he's saved by asking. You can reinforce the behaviors you want him to use, just like you can discourage the ones you don't want him to. In fact, it's even more effective since he's more likely to return. That works for all ages.

Offer a range of sources. Some children read over or under their grade level, and some don't look their age. Don't assume that one size fits all. It's likely that your waiting list for *Harry Potter* books included more than a few adults, and it's likely that children will want adult books even if they don't understand them entirely. Unless your library has rules and age restrictions, they have the right to check them out. Maybe that 10-year-old really does want to read Durant's philosophy books and will develop a lifelong interest. He'll never know if you don't allow him that freedom.

Children often have a hard time with search terms. Synonyms and "broader/narrower" are not easy concepts, and children can be very literal. If the assignment is about bluebirds, did the teacher mean the species, the Camp Fire Girls, or any bird that's blue? We have our suspicions, but the student may have already made up his mind. The context is key in a case like this, but convincing the child is another matter. Your best bet is just to tell him to come back if he needs more information.

READERS' TOOLS FOR CHILDREN

Children have their own interests outside their class work. That's true particularly for younger children and seems to diminish as they grow older. That may be an effect of finding their subject outside the library or online or having less time as their homework load grows. Recreational reading can encourage them to become lifelong learners or just give them a break from homework.

Readers' advisory for children is pretty much the same for children as adults, with the exception that it's difficult to tell a child's age and reading level by sight. A fifth grader may read at an adult level or at the first-grade level. The tall girl with makeup may only be 12, not an adult; the short tomboyish one may be 16. Like with adults, it's best to ask what a recent book they like was. That will give you a feel for what their level and interests are.

Subject reading lists and read-alikes work well with children if you put some thought into them. Just because the Arthurian legends and *Harry Potter* have magic and dragons doesn't mean they will appeal to the same readers, although they may. What is the part of one that they like? Is it the dragon, the magic, or that an orphaned boy becomes a hero?

Displays are a good way to group reading for children since you can select a number of books on a related topic or theme and children can select one that meets their needs and reading level. Children often make initial selections by the cover, so displays may attract them to titles they wouldn't otherwise look at. Any display or shelving that shows the covers will help children find something interesting.

Award winners are just that. They are good books but not for every child any more than an adult mystery reader will enjoy a Hugo-winning title. Children, especially tweens and teens, are more likely to pick their own book from a display than ask an "old person" for advice. Displays are their own advisory, particularly when organized around a theme. Don't neglect nonfiction; true stories and books targeted at a particular interest also have great appeal.

TWEENS AND TEENS

This is the age-group least likely to ask for help unless it's a homework assignment. Then they'd love you to do it—all of it. It's important to have guidelines in place for how much of the work you will do. It's good to have referrals to tutoring services in the community or volunteer tutors in the library.

They are also the group most likely to ask you questions that make you uncomfortable: questions about sex, pagan religions, homosexuality, their legal rights, and crime. Get over it. Most likely, they are curious. They saw something in a movie or on television, a friend told them something, or they are exploring their own sexual issues. They may just want to see if they can shock you through language, dress, or a number of piercings. That's almost a definition of "teenager," along with "Leave me alone."

It's generally better to let teens and tweens come to you. If you're in the stacks, a smile and a "Hi" may be all that you can do without getting "the scowl." Teens are very good at body language to show their feelings. If they respond, you can add, "If you need any help, I'm at the desk" or "Are you finding what you need?" Don't hang around if they don't respond, as they are used to being followed in retail stores and won't appreciate your presence. If you find them in the fiction section, you might add, "There's a display of good books that people have been reading by the desk" or some other relevant phrase.

TWEENS

Tweens are what used to be called "the awkward age," between ages 8 and 12. They're not kids, but they're not teens. They're old enough to be interested in what teens are interested in but not old enough to understand why they're interested.

They want to read what the teens are reading but are not emotionally prepared for the hard-edged real-life fiction that teens tend toward or the implications of what they read.

To make things more awkward, they're hovering around puberty. One week they want books about unicorns, the next they want graphic novels about murder, and the next perhaps books about homicidal unicorns.

They are very peer influenced, so if they ask for a book in a series, be sure you have them all. They will form their own informal book club and read them all. This is the age at which series are big hits, but the series will change every year. They also love books about celebrities, musicians, actors, and anyone else who could be a role model. The word "fan" is almost a synonym for "tween." Many of your reference questions will be about them.

Tweens are also thinking about their futures. Books about possible careers, from wife to archaeologist, are popular, and when they get interested in a topic, they want to read all about it, literally. Even though their reading levels may vary greatly, they are often willing to tackle a higher-level book on their interest. This means that they are the most unpredictable age-group you will serve. They are also the most rewarding. They are as smart as teens but don't have much attitude yet. That's the easy way to tell a teen from a tween.

You will have to find a level at which to conduct the reference interview, somewhere between a child and a teen. If you treat them like young adults, they will often live up to that idea. You can always lower the level of your questions if you see that they're not understanding you.

This is a good age for topical lists and displays since they can pick their own reading level from them. It's also good to have some books on similar topics and themes in the display since interests at this age change rapidly. They are also starting to feel independent, and selecting their own reading is a risk-free way to assert it.

TEENS

Teens get little enough privacy and respect, so give it to them at the library. You should anyway, but if they don't respond, give them their privacy. They are usually skilled computer users, if not skilled searchers, so you can offer an encouraging word in passing but don't hover.

Never call teens "teens" or "teenagers" to their faces. You might get away with "high schoolers" in a pinch, but if the teen isn't in school, that may alienate him. "Young adults" may sound patronizing, too. They think of themselves as almost adult, and indeed, they may have jobs and children, drive, vote, and do all the classic adult things. You can never insult a teen by implying he's older than he is.

Get assignments in advance, if possible, so tat you know what students need. Students will rarely bring the assignment with them and rarely remember exactly what they need. It also gives you a chance to be realistic with the teacher: databases aren't the same as Wikipedia or the Web; you don't subscribe to a lot of print journals anymore, so they can't just photocopy it; and your archives don't have what the National Archives have.

Never use closed questions with a teen if you want an answer. You may have to rephrase a question several times to get any response, so be patient. Nod often and use short, encouraging phrases, like "Right," "Okay," and "Uh-huh." Let him finish talking before you say anything longer so that he doesn't get an "Okay, now's when the adult tells me what to do" impression. Taking notes, even a word or two, is a sign that you're taking him seriously.

The library is a safe place for gays who are coming out to get information. No judgments should be made by staff. The patron already feels unwanted and different. Like other confidential interviews, you should have a quiet corner for consultations or at least walk them somewhere more private if the patron looks uncomfortable. You should have age-appropriate and culturally appropriate references, plus lists of local agencies, groups, clubs, and so on.

Have a lot of websites bookmarked on your Web page for this age-group. They are more likely to look than ask, especially for sensitive subjects. Have links to homework centers, tutoring centers, gaming groups, lesbian/gay/bigender/transsexual sources and organizations, and anything else that your teens ask about.

The reference interview will be somewhere between the adult and children's interview, with the addition of shrugs and raised eyebrows. Ignore those and be happy they're actually in the library. You'll see a lot more of them in online reference, as they live online and assume that everything they need is there.

Teens have an intellectual understanding of deadlines but may really care about them. After all, a recording label or talent scout might discover them tomorrow, so why sweat it? That may not be the truth, but it's the attitude they show. Teens are very peer influenced, so if their friends don't use the library, they won't, either. Anything that makes the library more attractive to them will give them an excuse to come. Gaming, music, Wi-Fi, or movies may not be what you want them to use, but it's not about you. And when you're not looking, they will look at graphic novels and even reference books.

Be consistent with teens. They will test your consistency and limits the same as they do any other authority figure. That's partly growing into an adult and partly hormones. Find a style that works, and stay with it both in conversation and in answering questions.

This is the age-group where you can use smileys and texting abbreviations in chat or e-mail. They grew up with them, and they expect them. Speed is more important to them than spelling, and they may be more formal with you as an "old person," but this is a chance to prove you have some element of understanding them. To a tween, there has always been texting and Twitter. Not knowing about them dates you to prehistory.

SENIORS

People over 65 are the fastest-growing group of patrons in the United States. They are also a vastly diverse group. Be careful not to stereotype them; some are raising grandchildren, some are still working, and some are marathon runners. Most have the same interests and hobbies they had when they were your age. They are also the most comfortable people in the physical library since that's what they grew up with.

A common problem is that they miss the card catalog and don't like using computers. When they see children happily surfing, they're even less likely to try to use them. This is a great point to turn your monitor so that they can see how you search and to tell them about classes in the library. If things are slow, you can demonstrate what's on your website.

Seniors will ask about many of the same subjects as teens, but the questions will be different. Teens may be interested in famous true crimes, seniors about crime in their neighborhood. Have some handouts and a Web page for both seniors and those who care for them with links to information on Social Security, health care, housing, and local and national agencies. You will use it too since senior patrons may be reluctant to.

Seniors are more likely to use the phone for reference questions since it's the technology they're most comfortable with and most have. More seniors are likely to be homebound than the general population. Consider having a separate line for seniors' questions, perhaps in an office where there are fewer noises to compete with your voice. Train your bookmobile staff to do reference interviews and at least to fill out a form so that you send materials on the next run or call the patron back.

PROBLEM PATRONS

If you've worked in retail, you've encountered them. If you've shopped retail, you've seen them. These are problem customers who use language to berate and intimidate the employees whose job is to make patrons happy. The customer is always right.

Luckily, you have more choices than that poor employee, who must take the abuse because he has no alternative. You have skills to deal with him and alternatives to endure abuse. You have policies.

The proverbial problem patron may also belong to any other group you serve. He may be a patron who has a problem outside the library and may annoy people all over town. He may have a legitimate complaint with service. He may be an eccentric who does nothing wrong but takes up all your time. The patrons may not be problems, but your and the library's attitudes may be. In any case, you need some special skills to cope with them.

As the environment and services that libraries offer change, so will the issues. The patron with a laptop who keys too loud for another patron, the students working on a group project, the person on his cell phone, and the programming right out in the library and not tucked into a corner room are all facts of life that some patrons will have a hard time with. Change happens all the time. These may be your most common complaints but not the most difficult to deal with.

You may have unattended children, exhibitionists, vandals, and arsonists. These are real problems. The rest are basically people who make other people uncomfortable. Libraries, not just public ones but state universities and community colleges, are tax supported and should give the same services to all the public, whether they are taxpayers or not.

It is also part of the American Library Association code. You serve all your patrons, not just the quiet ones, the polite ones, or the ones who smell pleasant. You don't get to decide who is worthy of your services.

Be very careful about judging patrons by their looks. The dirty, sweaty guy may just have come from a football practice; the drooling, slurring patron may have had a stroke; and the wild-eyed woman may have 10 kids and five minutes to get something to read. Librarians, of all people, should know better than to judge a book by its cover.

Patrons with mental illnesses deserve your services, too. It may take more of your time to get to the real question and more of your patience, but they have real information needs as well. They may be annoying. Don't take it personally. That problem patron is probably a problem at the grocery store and church. People with mental illness aren't doing things on purpose to annoy you or anyone else. It's a symptom of their illness.

Librarians often say that they are not social workers and that they are neither trained nor paid for that job. In reality, your library should train you in simple useful skills because you work with all the public, not just the polite ones. Big-box stores do that much training; it's part of customer service. Big-box stores might have more backup for the person on the front lines, though, in the form of security guards and managers. One thing your library should provide is a line of command for such situations. The reference desk is the face of the library, the most accessible area and the one where patrons have a real person to talk to: you. That is part of the job, even if it's one you didn't expect in library school.

Not all problem patrons are major problems. The guy who talks too loud on his cell phone, the woman who thinks she's a librarian, and the running child can all be handled by referring to your rules. People have lived with rules for a long time, and most get the concept. Follow the rules or leave. It's the same situation at retail stores, parks, churches, schools, and your parent's house. You may not like the rules—they may in fact be unreasonable—but they are the rules. Have a copy that you can give the patron, have them posted by your doors, and read them to children when you need to enforce them.

Here again there are lessons to be learned from other fields, including retail and business (Sarkodie-Mensah 2002). If you want more training, talk to people in other fields, as they have the same patrons with the same issues but other ideas and often more experience. Talk to other agencies in your area and talk among yourselves. You might even want to have a meeting with all your "problem" patrons, a chance to let them air their complaints and get some feedback from their viewpoint.

There are webinars offered by Web Junction and business groups, there are workshops offered by colleges, and there are videos on YouTube. There are books and articles from many fields: social work, medicine, law enforcement, and retail.

There are resources on all kinds of people skills and management skills besides problems, too. Don't overlook what other people can teach you.

SKILLS FOR PROBLEM PATRONS

Body language can give your patron a message. That message can be that you are timid or confident. You want to give the message that you are confident and in control of the situation. Stand tall and don't rush when you walk. Don't shift your weight from foot to foot or fidget. Stay about an arm's length away from the patron to give both of you personal space.

Keep your voice level and calm; a shaky voice is a major clue that you are nervous. You can try an old teacher's trick and keep your voice pitched low and very quiet. That often makes the patron lower his voice to hear you.

If all this is not natural for you, you can try an actor's trick and become someone else. Do you know a teacher or nurse who can calm and control people just by her presence? She has those same characteristics, and you can simply pretend that you are her. That doesn't mean doing an impersonation; simply ask yourself, "What would Miss Jones do?" That can give you the confidence and tone that you feel you lack.

Some libraries allow a little leeway in handling complaints. Is there a different way you can help the patron? Can you get the book on interlibrary loan? Do you have the authority to bend a rule? If you can't resolve the problem, refer him to someone higher up in the library. You will want to know who to refer him to and warn them before sending the patron. That person may never show up, but the threat may be enough to change his behavior.

Give the patron something to do about their issue. You should have a complaint form; give him one and tell him what to do with it when he's done. Just taking an action means that you take it seriously. That may be enough. It may actually trigger a review of the policy if enough people complain about the same thing. Just because someone has an issue doesn't mean he doesn't have a point.

If a patron has several complaints, try to find one you can act on and concentrate on it. That shows that you are taking the issue seriously. If you can't do that, isolate the behavioral issue and resolve that before you move on to others. That makes the conversation conditional on his behavior, not yours. "If you will stop shouting, we can discuss this" gives him an action to take even if it's not one he wants. You can continue to discuss issues in still smaller sections. Finding a resolution to one issue or one part of an issue will usually defuse the patron enough to have a calmer conversation.

DISRUPTIVE PATRONS

Sometimes the patron will be disruptive. Disruptive isn't the same as violent, but your other patrons may be uncomfortable with the situation. You want to control the situation before another patron tries to step in. Listen carefully to complaints. It shows that you take them seriously. Don't agree or disagree with him, though. Stay neutral. You can't control the patron's behavior, but you can control your response. By being calm and neutral, you are setting an example of what you mean. Take a deep breath, count to 10, but keep listening.

Try phrasing things to relate to disturbing other patrons. Tell the patron that his behavior is making the other patrons feel uncomfortable. Peer pressure may be more effective than a stance of authority.

You can say, "I'm sorry you feel that way" or "That must be frustrating." You acknowledge his feelings without agreeing with his statement. He may take it as an apology, but that's okay. Don't apologize for the library, yourself, or your policies, though. Just acknowledge his feelings.

Don't be confrontational; just repeat the policy. Have your policies on paper so that you can hand them to a patron: they're in a library because they trust the authority of paper, so that may turn the trick. Or maybe not. Use your policies as a framework for solutions: these are the rules; do you agree to follow them? Phrasing things in terms of rules puts them into a familiar context; explain that if the patron doesn't follow the rules, he can't stay. You can soften that by saying that he's welcome to come back when he can follow them. That takes it out of a personal issue and makes it a behavioral one.

By confronting the patron, you can escalate the problem. Remember, he may not be entirely responsible for the behavior. No one wants to be told that, though, or be confronted in public. Try to talk to him in a semiprivate area, as you want to be able to summon help if it's needed.

If a situation escalates, keep something physically between you and the patron. If you can, keep something between him and other patrons, too. Have a panic button or hotline for emergencies. Even a cheap pay-as-you-go cell phone with 911 on speed dial will work. If you can't get someone to back you up, what will you do? Can you walk away, ask a patron for help, or call a person up the chain of command? Knowing in advance will make your decision easier.

If a situation escalates to threats of violence or if the patron becomes verbally abusive or actually becomes violent, it's time to take more extreme action. Call your security guard (if you have one) or call the police. Those acts are actually illegal. The library may not press charges, but they are grounds to call the police. You have a duty to protect patrons as well as serve them.

There are some warning signs you can look for. If the patron gets uncomfortably close, seems agitated, looks pale, or sweats a great deal, these may be signs that the encounter will get violent. They may also be signs that he is epileptic and is about to have a seizure, so don't assume that violence is likely.

If the patron seems to be gathering allies, don't let yourself be surrounded. It's time to call in backup of some kind. Just another librarian approaching may disperse them; they may just be curious, but situations such as this can escalate when the patron has an audience.

It's also a trouble sign if the patron shouts, threatens, or pounds the table. Those aren't necessarily signs that he will attack you, but they are disruptive, and you should call in backup again.

Don't touch the patron. That can be construed as an attack and in reality can lead to assault charges, assault being touching someone against his or her will.

Have a form that you can fill out for incidents that go beyond a simple resolution. You can send that to other staff members or shifts and keep a copy for your records. Documentation has several purposes. It gives you facts if you need to take an action like banning a patron, it gives you a record to bring to higher-ups and show what you deal with, and it can spur actions and policies that will deter the problem in the future. Consult with an attorney or the police about what documentation you need and what you should keep so that you have what you need for action.

HOMELESS PATRONS

In both urban and rural communities, there are people who are homeless. They are your patrons, too. Sometimes homelessness is a result of economic problems and sometimes social ones, and sometimes the disheveled patron has just come from a marathon. Maybe the man who stays all day is retired and dreamed of spending his days surrounded by books. Once again, don't judge the book by its cover.

Many homeless shelters are closed during daylight hours, when libraries are open. Libraries are warm, safe places where there are things to do. Children are also homeless, so they may come with their parent. It can be useful to have a handout with resources for homeless people of all ages, with library resources as well as social ones. Books are quiet time filler in a library, but you may want to invite them to informational sessions and programming.

Other patrons may complain about your homeless ones, sometimes for silly reasons. Toddlers can be smelly, loud, and sleeping in the library, but no one calls them a problem patron group who should be banned (Hersberger 2005). It's useful to have a pair of handouts you can give the patrons: one for those who complain, explaining what the library policy is on the homeless, and one for the homeless that includes what resources are available in the library. If you have a friends group, talk to them about what the issues are and what the library can do about them. A basket of inexpensive grooming and hygiene needs in the restrooms so that patrons don't have to come to the reference desk and ask can solve many of the issues, and your friends group may have contacts to get them donated.

REFERENCES

Hersberger, J. A. "The Homeless and Information Needs and Services." *Reference & User Services Quarterly* 44, no. 3 (2005): 199–202.
Sarkodie-Mensah, Kwasi, ed. *Helping the Difficult Library Patron: New Approaches to Examining and Resolving a Long-Standing and On-Going Problem.* New York: Haworth, 2002.

FURTHER READING

American Library Association. "Guidelines for Library Services to Spanish-Speaking Library Users." *Reference & User Services Quarterly* 47, no. 2 (Winter 2007): 194–97.

Avery, Susan. "When Opportunity Knocks: Opening the Door through Teachable Moments." *The Reference Librarian* 49, no. 2 (2008): 109–18.

Bishop, Kay, and Anthony Salveggi. "Responding to Developmental Stages in Reference Service to Children." *Public Libraries* 40, no. 6 (2001): 354–58.

Blessinger, K. D. "Problem Patrons: All Shapes and Sizes." *The Reference Librarian* 36, no. 75 (2002): 3–10.

Bosman, Ellen, John P. Bradford, and Robert Gay Ridinger. *Lesbian, Bisexual, and Transgendered Literature: A Genre Guide.* Westport CT: Libraries Unlimited, 2008.

Burton, Melvin. "Reference Interview: Strategies for Children." *North Carolina Libraries* 56, no. 3 (1998): 110–13.

Chelton, M. K. "The 'Problem Patron' Public Libraries Created." *The Reference Librarian* 36, no. 75 (2002): 23–32.

Curry, Ann. "If I Ask, Will They Answer? Evaluating Public Library Reference Service to Gay and Lesbian Youth." *Reference & User Services Quarterly* 45, no. 1 (Fall 2005): 165.

Flowers, Sarah. "Guidelines for Library Services to Teens." *Young Adult Library Services* 6, no. 3 (Spring 2008): 4, 6–7.

Holt, Glen E., and Leslie E. Holt. "Setting and Applying Appropriate Rules Governing Patron Behaviour." *Public Library Quarterly* 24, no. 1 (2005): 73–85.

Jones, Patrick. *New Directions for Library Service to Young Adults.* Chicago: American Library Association, 2002.

Lexile.com. http://www.lexile.com/findabook/StudentInfo.aspx. Search for a book by Lexile score/range and subject matter.

Library of Virginia Notable Books. http://www.lva.virginia.gov/lib-edu/LDND/lexile. The Notable Books list is annotated with lexile scores, sortable by all fields.

Long, Sarah Ann. "Serving the 'Boomer' Generation and Beyond." *New Library World* (London) 106, no. 7–8 (2005): 378–90.

Mabry, Celia Hales. "Serving Seniors: Dos and Don'ts at the Desk." *American Libraries* 34, no. 11 (December 2003): 64–65.

Ohio Reference Excellence. http://www.olc.org/ore/index.html (accessed October 21, 2010).

Osa, J. O. "The Difficult Patron Situation: Competency-Based Training to Empower Frontline Staff." *The Reference Librarian* 36, no. 75 (2002): 265–78.

Rubin, Rhea Joyce. *Defusing the Angry Patron: A How-to-Do-It Manual for Librarians and Paraprofessionals.* New York: Neal-Schuman, 2000.

Steele, Anitra T. *Bare Bones Children's Services: Tips for Public Library Generalists.* Chicago: American Library Association, 2001.

Sullivan, Michael. *Fundamentals of Children's Services.* Chicago: ALA Editions, 2005.

Thompson, Samantha H. "The Pixilated Problem Patrons: Or, the Trials of Working Virtual Reference and What We've Learned from It." *The Reference Librarian* 50, no. 3 (2009): 291–96.

Willis, Mark R. *Dealing with Difficult People in the Library.* Chicago: American Library Association, 1999.

3 CULTURAL DIFFERENCES

There are few areas where you will work with people from only one culture. Some areas are predominantly one national heritage, but that doesn't mean it's the only one. Nor does national heritage mean culture; there are many differences between urban and rural populations and many more between religious or regional groups. Once you could count on people from one region sharing a language or maybe two, but modern travel makes that an outdated assumption.

Any time you find yourself thinking of people as "other," think of your own family. Most of us are only a few generations descended from immigrants who had the same problems newcomers have now. A new language, a new culture, a new lifestyle—they all faced the same challenges. You've faced some of them, too. Were you a punk in your teens? Goth? Did people avoid you and treat you like an alien? Practice your empathy skills with someone who knew you then.

You can't assume that sharing a cultural background means that they share personal characteristics. It may be true that both Muslim and Amish women dress modestly, but that tells you only about what they wear. It doesn't tell you anything about them as people or about their culture. Don't stereotype people—and that's what you're doing when you make judgments of a group. If someone self-identifies as Goth, that doesn't mean he's not an engineering student; someone who self-identifies as an army veteran may be looking for an opera score. Don't limit people by their cultural or national identification.

Don't ignore that self-identification, though. There's a difference between self-identification and your identification. They know what they're saying, and you're putting words in their mouths. That will, consciously or unconsciously, make a difference in how you conduct the reference interview. You're interviewing this individual, not a group; self-identification gives you some clues as to what the social aspect will be, but you need the reference interview even more to find out what this person's real question is.

Remember that you self-identify, too. You self-identify as a librarian, but librarians have many roles in a library, and each has a different background. Do you hate being called "Marian the Librarian" and being told that you don't look like a librarian? Do you hate being told that you can't possibly understand someone's point of view because you aren't part of their group? Think of that when you feel yourself thinking, "Here comes the (fill in the blank)." Empathy is an essential skill in dealing with people.

WELCOMING NEW PATRONS

Welcoming patrons from other cultures is as important as answering their questions. Don't think you don't have any patrons from other cultures. If you don't, you need to make your library welcoming to them. Although we often think of other cultures as being other countries, there are many other factors related to cultures. Culture includes folkways, foods, music, child rearing, marriage, religion, and all the things that make us human. Every group has a different group of characteristics that make up a culture. Most but not all of those characteristics are shared. People are hard to pigeonhole, so don't even try.

The first step of the reference interview is being welcoming, and that's even more important when your patron comes from another culture. Patrons may fear that their English will be misunderstood or ridiculed. They may have been ignored for their appearance. This may have happened in retail settings, making them more reluctant to ask for something in a library, where the stakes are higher.

You can be proactively welcoming, inviting patrons to ask questions. Don't assume that patrons know you will do that or what information is available. You should have handouts and flyers in your patrons' languages and have them available wherever your patrons go. That means anyplace that will take them: medical facilities, community centers, churches, schools, stores, youth centers, orientation sessions, and festival booths. They should be prominently displayed as close to your front door as possible, even in an outdoor box, such as those that real estate agents use for flyers in front of a house.

In their culture or area, libraries may not be like yours. They may be only in big cities or may hold only nonfiction, with patrons expected to buy fiction reading elsewhere. Books may be so rare that none circulate, and the very concept may be new to them. Libraries may be subscription based; many libraries around the world started this way. They may be associated with colleges and available only to students. They may share information about what a patron reads or require proof of residency to use the library. There are many social and psychological barriers to using a library. That's only one of the reasons that outreach efforts are so important. Patrons may not realize that your library is their library, too.

In still other cultures, especially in the former Soviet bloc, patrons may challenge librarians. Sometimes that may be a sense of freedom—that they can do so without risking consequences. Sometimes it's the memories of how incorrect state information could be. Their behavior may strike you as rude, but it isn't.

It's learned from their experiences. It's not personal, and you may want to teach them how to check information against other sources to verify it. That's a teachable moment.

We know that some people see asking for help as imposing on an important person (you) or admitting defeat. That's even more common in some other cultures where authority is simply not challenged. People in authority are treated with great courtesy even when wrong. In others, education is held in high esteem, and someone with a degree is assumed to be correct or to already know everything important. In some, where libraries are rare, librarians are seen as keepers of knowledge who are not inclined to share such a valuable commodity. All those reasons can lead people to avoid libraries and librarians.

Prominent displays on other cultures may draw people into your library, if only to correct you. You can partner with community organizations in these and offer programming that ties into them. Plan them around curricular calendars so that students and patrons can mix. Nothing is more welcoming than seeing your friends somewhere.

Don't make any assumptions about these patrons anymore than you would with others. You can be very embarrassed when the heavily accented patron turns out to be your new boss or doctor. He may have lived in your country for years, he may be a graduate student, or he may be a new arrival. He may keep the traditional dress from home for decades with pride. He may keep traditional speech habits in English. Don't assume that means he doesn't know our culture.

Only a few ethnic groups are native to any area. The rest of us are descendants of immigrants who faced the same issues that new arrivals do now. Be as open minded and welcoming to them as you would to your ancestors.

WELCOME TO YOUR LIBRARY!

You can start welcoming patrons by literally doing just that. Exterior signage should be in whatever languages are common in your area. If you've traveled abroad, you've seen signs that say "English spoken here" and gone there first. Even if the English is spoken poorly, you know you're welcome. Have at least handouts of your floor plans translated so that you can point to things and not struggle with the terms. Translate as many of your handouts as you can and have them someplace where patrons don't have to ask for them. Have a "Questions? Ask us here" map on it with the location of the reference desk shown. Even better, have a podcast or tape explaining your library and your procedures made by a native speaker. MP3 players are inexpensive, and you may still have cassette players around your library. This is a great chance to use them again.

There can be large differences in body language between cultures. Eye contact has different meanings in different cultures, especially between men and women. Eye contact may have sexual connotations that aren't intended and may be perceived as challenging or even hostile. That's one of the reasons for not holding eye contact too long. Shifting from eye to eye or from eye to center of the forehead doesn't send those messages. You want to look interested—but only in the question and not the patron.

If the patron is uncomfortable and nervous, it will show in his body language but perhaps not in the way you expect. He may gesture more, trying to show you what he means. He may become very still, withdrawing from the interaction. The important thing is to notice the change. Follow his lead in changing your body language but make yours more attentive. You may want to try open questions again at this point since you may well have missed the point of the question.

You also want to mirror the terms he uses before you rephrase a question. An option that Americans seldom think of, as we are such a monolingual culture, is to use a term in a third language if you know one. Many countries, especially in Europe, have several languages, and most people pick up at least a few words and phrases. It's also helpful to have a cheat sheet of frequently used phrases in several languages, such as "I need more information" and "Is this answer your question?" Either of you can point to what you want to say.

Personal space is different, too. Don't be surprised if a patron moves away from you or doesn't want to be touched. In fact, avoid touching patrons at all since it can often be misinterpreted in any culture. On the other hand, some cultures have different limits on personal space and may get closer than you are comfortable with. That's showing not sexual interest but rather personal interest in what you're saying. If you're not comfortable, you can take a step backward or direct the patron to the materials you're looking at.

There are age and gender issues, too. In some cultures, one simply does not bother one's seniors, certainly not with trivial questions like where to find something. Maybe it's traditional to ask a senior family member before asking a stranger. Perhaps men don't ask women or vice versa. If a patron goes out of his way to ask someone else, don't take it personally.

Some cultures are not demonstrative and don't show emotion to strangers. If a patron doesn't smile, it may be a cultural trait and not that he's unhappy with you or doesn't understand you. On the other hand, the patron may be confused and not show it or may mask it with a smile.

THE QUESTION

The question will be the hard part of the interview if you don't share a language and the assumptions that come from living in a certain culture. That's not limited to different languages, either. If someone asks an American for a book on knitting jumpers, the American will be puzzled, while an Australian will know that means what Americans call sweaters.

The first and most important thing that you can convey to the patron is that not knowing is okay. It's okay not to speak fluently, it's okay not to know the answer, and it's okay to ask for help. The phrase "That's what I'm here for" may be the most used one in reference. We usually don't know, either, but we know where to look. Even if we know, we'll show the source to prove it. The reference interview is for people to ask what they don't know so that the patron fits right in with the rest of your patrons. Let him know that.

When a language is taught in a school, it's the most formal and correct version, which most people don't speak in their daily lives. When a language is learned from a native speaker, the accent is often learned as well. An opera singer may have learned German from a Pole, while a Haitian may have learned English from a Frenchman. Don't let the accent deceive you; the patron may not speak the language but may have the accent. Slang and idioms are seldom taught in formal settings, either, so avoid them. In addition, they don't translate well, as you tend to translate the literal and not the casual meaning, leading to more misunderstandings. "From the horse's mouth" or "true blue" are easy to translate, but the meaning doesn't come with the words. English is a complex language that borrows words from many other languages but changes the meanings of those words, and accents differ even within a state in the United States.

That's true of other languages, too. If you speak a little French, the idioms and slang will still confuse you. Expect both to ask the patron to rephrase his question and to be asked to do the same.

Speaking and comprehension skills are two different things, using two different parts of the brain. A patron who speaks little English may understand much more and vice versa. Television shows and movies in English are a staple around the world, so the patron may be very familiar with the language and understand it but have had few chances to speak it. In some countries, English is taught like Latin—from the book, with a great deal of reading but no chances to speak it.

Confusion about names is common. Some cultures place family names first, in some women keep their maiden names, and in others a name may be used socially but not legally. We then add to that confusion by talking about Henry Lee but cataloging him as Lee, Henry. Then we compound it by referring to him as General Lee, Henry Lee III, Harry Lee, or Light Horse Henry Lee, not to be confused with Robert E. Lee or Dark Horse Lee. You can see why anyone would need help clarifying which Lee they need and the order of the names. Ask for the family name, not the last name.

That's true for both the reference question and the questions about the patron. When you take notes to pass a question on or answer it later, make sure that you have the names in the right order or underline the family name. Imagine your embarrassment when you ask for the equivalent of "Mrs. Maryanne" and are corrected. It doesn't inspire confidence in the accuracy of your answer.

Don't use complex questions or either/or choices. Use short questions and phrase either/or as two separate questions. Answering for two questions at once is stressful, and if the patron understands one part and not the other, you'll go back to separate questions again to find which is which. Avoid negative questions like "You didn't want to do this, did you?" They just lead to more confusion.

So do complex sentences. Use a few short sentences instead. It's easier to understand single sentences than to decipher a complex one. Avoid long verb forms, too. "I will be looking for that" is more confusing than "I will look for that." The meaning is slightly different but not enough to justify the confusion it can cause.

Don't use slang or jargon. Remember, jargon is still another language. If you need to use jargon, you can consult a website and find the translation, but that still means that your patron has to know what you're taking about to start with. If the patron knows the term, he will often say so as you explain it. If he doesn't know it, you'll have to explain it anyway.

Avoid contractions, which often aren't taught in language classes. They are often also confusingly similar. "Your" and "you're," "he'll" and "heel," and "its" and "it's" are all too similar to distinguish when you're concentrating on the content, but the words don't seem to fit the context. Formal is better than casual when the patron may not know idioms and contractions, even if it feels a little strange to you.

EFFECTIVE LISTENING

Attitudes are a large part of effectively listening to a nonnative speaker. If you know people with accents, you are more likely to put some effort into understanding, even if the person you know has a Texas accent and the person you are talking to has an Irish one. If you speak another language, it's easier to understand a foreign accent, even if it's not the language you know, because you have trained your brain. Concentrate on the meaning and not the pronunciation.

You may think that it's difficult to understand accented English. It is, as it takes more concentration and perhaps longer to process. The patron is having the same problem with you. This may lead to pauses in speech for either of you while you think or mentally translate. Don't assume that the patron is done speaking or doesn't understand unless the pause becomes protracted.

Spanish speakers often add an "e" before a final "s," Russians may pronounce "v" as "w," Japanese speakers may reverse "l" and "r" and Arabs "p" and "b," and there is no "z" sound in Norwegian, so they use an "s." Knowing these tendencies may make it easier for you to understand your patrons.

Context is helpful when listening. You can mentally fill in the blanks if you know what you're discussing. Be sure to give your patron enough context to do the same. If you pay attention to the context, you can often get enough of the question to fill in the blanks. If not, repeat what you understand and let the patron help you with the rest. Between the two of you, you can often work the rest out.

Spanish is the most frequent second language in large parts of the United States. There are 45 political units in South America, and "Hispanic" relates only to Spanish-speaking people. Mexico has diversity among even that population; some are from Spain, some are Native Americans, and some are from other European countries. Nor does coming from South America mean that you speak Spanish at all, as there are dozens of native languages, and the official language of Brazil is Portuguese. It's helpful to find out more specifics before starting the interview (Amsberry 2009).

You can try one of the online translation services, like Babel Fish or Google Translate, to get the essence of a question and answer. Google Translate will even read the sentence in the language. The translation won't be perfect; it may well be pidgin, but that's the purpose of pidgin: to bridge two languages. Hopefully, you have made contact with a local community organization in advance and can call to get a translation in real time. You may have staff who speak a second language, too, or student assistants who are bilingual. This is a good thing to keep in your intranet or wiki so that you have a place to go for help.

If you speak too fast, you may leave your patron far behind the conversation. Don't exaggerate, but do speak slowly enough for your patron to follow you. Own your language problems, too; you can apologize for not understanding without losing face. After all, it's your job to talk to the patron, not vice versa. Americans are notorious for not speaking other languages and expecting others to speak English, so an apology would be a welcoming act in itself.

You can write your conversation down and use a language-to-language dictionary to get the words right. It may take a while, especially with technical terms, to get through the question and the interview process, but it's worth it. It's common for a family member to help the patron translate (Chu 1999). You can treat that like any other "imposed" question and speak to the real patron while the family member translates for both of you.

Don't assume that something is "common knowledge" with a patron who is not a native English speaker. Much of what we learn in elementary school and at home is specific to our home country or region. Take a minute to explain anything that isn't self-evident. Daniel Boone may be well known in the mid-South but not in Alaska and totally unknown in Asia. On the other hand, you may not be able to name a single figure in Bolivian history, and a Bolivian patron will think you're ignorant.

Patrons may not realize the difference between "could," "should," and "must." The connotations that they are an option, a suggestion, and a requirement are subtle and not often taught in classes, so take a minute to clarify them. "You could, if you want to . . . ," "I suggest that you . . . ," and "We require that you . . . ," make them clearer, but be prepared to rephrase them again. After all, what is an option in your library may be an absolute requirement elsewhere, and the patron may think that he has misunderstood your meaning based on his experience.

The online translation services have the same problem. "I want to find out" translates to and back from German as "I must know." They have the same meaning but different connotations. One sounds curious, the other demanding or desperate. If a patron mentally translates from his own language, he may sound demanding or demeaning. That's the same case as "must" and "could" in reverse. English has no gender, so don't be surprised by odd sentence constructions or what you consider demeaning to women. It may be an idiom that's well known and often used in his native language but that translates badly. "Mon petit doigt me l'a dit"—"my little finger told me"—is just as bizarre to us as "a little bird told me" is to a Frenchman. Neither means what it says. In this case, it may not be important, but a "capote anglaise" (English hood) and a French letter are not what they seem (although they mean the same thing: a condom), and you probably don't want to suggest either to a patron looking for a costume piece or Voltaire's correspondence.

Use humor sparingly. Not every culture has the same sense of humor, finds it appropriate for librarians, or finds it suitable between sexes. It's another case where the literal translation is not what you want to say. If you use humor, it's best to use it at your own expense and never at the expense of patrons. Jokes don't translate well.

Be certain that the patron has given you the whole question before you decide that you don't understand it. Sometimes the last word or phrase is the one that makes it all click. He may be giving you the information need in the order of his own language instead of yours. The noun or verb may be far separated from each other and meet only at the end of the sentence. That's the point where you can restate it and watch for agreement.

You watch for signs of agreement because many people will nod when they don't understand or to be pleasant. If you suspect that, ask the patron to restate the question. That may feel awkward when you're used to doing it yourself, but you can phrase it another way. "Is there anything else I should know? Okay, what have we agreed on?" can do the trick.

THE ANSWER

Remember what you've already learned about questions when you give the answer: short sentences, no idioms, and no slang. You have an advantage with answers since you now have something you can just point at to refer to it.

Always give the patron the call number or the source in writing. He may be reluctant to ask you to repeat or spell it, so be sure that he leaves with at least the correct source without trying to remember it in another language. That should be a general practice, but it's doubly important when your patron is bilingual or from another culture. Don't overload your patron with too much to remember.

Non-Roman and Asian alphabets may need another character set to be read, and this should be available on the desktop in the library. Most browsers have built-in support for the text in other character sets. Helping a patron who is reading in them or searching in them can be a problem, though. This is a good time to call in your backups or to talk in English and let him do the searching. It's not an optimal solution, but it does indicate that you're interested and helpful if not able to help him yourself.

Couch your answers in plain English. You can speak it even if you're a librarian. Avoid complicated sentence structures and contractions unless your patron has used them and obviously understands them. You don't have to speak especially slowly, but do leave a little time between sentences so that your patron has time to mentally translate them. Once again, you can rephrase your answer like you did the patron's question to be sure that you understand each other.

Don't ask, "Do you understand?" Polite people will nod and smile, even if they don't, to be polite or respectful. Make it an open-ended question instead. You can ask them to repeat what you've said to confirm their understanding. If you rephrased their question in the interview, they'll have an idea of what you're doing. This may be the point where you invite the patron to come back if he needs more help. That gives him a graceful out if you really have got it all wrong.

If patrons seem reluctant to go into the stacks, that may be because they aren't allowed to in their home country. Reassure them and take them there. Where all books are rare, browsing and circulation are also. Your patron may have no idea of self-service, borrowing books, interlibrary loan, or reserves/holds. You may want to have a staff member accompany them or give them a general tour if you can't leave the desk.

Taking patrons to the stacks also gives them a chance to see how the stacks are organized. Stack browsing has fallen out of favor in the world of online public access catalogs, but it's a good way to introduce the patron to it. It also gives him a chance to browse nearby call numbers if he sees something else of interest.

You may feel challenged and frustrated working with these patrons, but you shouldn't show it. These are your newest patrons, and you should put effort not only into answering their questions, which may be a new experience for them, but also into making the library a welcoming and safe experience.

Take your chance to invite them back. They may not realize that the desk is staffed regularly or that someone else could help them. Be sure they leave with your handouts, in their language or not, and a map of the library. Tell them about upcoming programs and events. Show them where your bulletin boards and the public access computers are. These patrons may not know that you offer more than reference services and books. Literally inviting them back for more tells them that you're not the only friendly and helpful person in the library and that there's much more than books there.

SAMPLE INTERVIEWS

> Please, I need help with rats.
> Okay, what do you need to know about rats?
> I must know what they eat and where they sleep. They run all over the house.
> Can you tell me more about what you need?
> Yes, do they swim? I must know that.
> All right, you need to know what they eat, where they sleep, and whether they can swim. Is that all?
> Shampoo. I must know if you can wash the rats.
> So you need to know what they eat, where they sleep, whether they can swim, and if they can be washed. Is that correct?

Yes. My son brings home rats from school and does not know to how care of them. I must know. I do not like them, but I must know.

So you need something for your son. How old is your son?

He is seven. He is too young for pets.

Let me check the catalog. We have "How to care for your pet rats." Does that sound like what you need? It has photographs, too. Okay, let's go look at it.

Can I help you find something?

Yes, but I cannot talk here. There are people here.

Okay, let's walk over here. It's quieter here.

My daughter has women's problem. I need a book for her.

What kind of problem does she have?

Women's problem. You know. She is 12, she has women's problem.

Your daughter is 12, and she has a woman's problem. Has she started her monthly periods?

I do not know. We do not talk about it. Her mother is dead. She needs a book.

All right, your daughter is 12 and needs a book about reaching womanhood?

Yes. Becoming a woman.

Okay, we have several books. We also have some videos on the subject, if you think she would like to hear someone explain.

I do not want to hear. A book.

All right, we have several books about becoming a woman. Maybe she would like to have more than one?

More is good.

All right, let's walk over and look at them.

No. I cannot go there. You bring them here.

Okay, I can't leave the desk right now. Would it be okay if a page gets them and takes them to the checkout for you? You can get them on your way out.

Yes. That is good. I brought a bag.

All right, then Nancy will take them there. Just ask for the books Nancy brought there. If your daughter needs to know more, tell her she can call or come in and look for more books. Any of the librarians can help her find more, but my name is Susie, if she wants to ask for me. Is there anything else I can help you find?

No. This is good. She reads good, she will be happy now.

REFERENCES

Amsberry, Dawn. "Using Effective Listening Skills with International Patrons." *Reference Services Review* 37, no. 1 (2009): 10–19.

Chu, Clara M. "Immigrant Children Mediators (ICM): Bridging the Literacy Gap in Immigrant Communities." Paper presented at the 65th IFLA Council and General Conference, Bangkok, Thailand, August 20–August 28, 1999.

FURTHER READING

ACRL Instruction Section. "Multilingual Glossary." http://www.ala.org/ala/mgrps/divs/acrl/about/sections/is/projpubs/multilingual.cfm (accessed October 21, 2010).

American Library Association. "Guidelines for Library Services to Spanish-Speaking Library Users." http://www.ala.org/ala/mgrps/divs/rusa/resources/guidelines/guidespanish.cfm (accessed October 20, 2010).

Badke, William. "International Students: Information Literacy or Academic Literacy." *Academic Exchange Quarterly* 6, no. 4 (Winter 2002): 60–66.

Baron, Sara, and Alexia Strout-Dapaz. "Communicating with and Empowering International Students with a Library Skills Set." *Reference Services Review* 29, no. 4 (2001): 314–26.

Brown, C. C. "Reference Services to the International Adult Learner: Understanding the Barriers." *The Reference Librarian* 69/70 (2000): 337–47.

Conteh-Morgan, Miriam. "Connecting the Dots: Limited English Proficiency, Second Language Learning Theories, and Information Literacy Instruction." *Journal of Academic Librarianship* 28, no. 4 (July/August 2002): 191–96.

Cuban, S. *Serving New Immigrant Communities in the Library.* Westport, CT: Libraries Unlimited, 2007.

Dali, Keren. "Readers' Advisory Interactions with Immigrant Readers." *New Library World* 111, no. 5/6 (2010): 213–22.

de Souza, Y. "Reference Work with International Students: Making the Most Use of the Neutral Question." *Reference Services Review* 24, no. 4 (1996): 41–48.

DiMartino, D. J., and L. R. Zoe. "International Students and the Library: New Tools, New Users, and New Instruction." In *Teaching the New Library to Today's Users,* edited by T. Jacobsen and H. C. Williams, 17–43. New York: Neal-Schuman, 2000.

Emson, S. "Canadian Public Library Services to Newcomers: Challenges for the Saskatoon Public Library." http://atwork.settlement.org/downloads/atwork/INSCAN_Spring2009_Canadian_Public_Library_Services_to_Newcomers.pdf (accessed October 25, 2010).

Ferrer-Vinenta, Ignacio J. "For English, Press 1: International Students' Language Preference at the Reference Desk." *The Reference Librarian* 51, no. 3 (July 2010): 189–201.

Hall-Ellis, S. D. "Subject Access for Readers' Advisory Services: Their Impact on Contemporary Spanish Fiction in Selected Public Library Collections." *Public Library Quarterly* 27, no. 1 (2008): 1–18.

Jiao, Qun G., and Anthony J. Onwuebguzie. "Sources of Library Anxiety among International Students." *Urban Library Journal* 11, no. 1 (Fall 2001): 16–27.

Kumar, S. L., and R. S. Suresh. "Strategies for Providing Effective Reference Services for International Adult Learners." *The Reference Librarian* 69 (2000): 327–36.

Liestman, Daniel. "Reference Services and the International Adult Learner." *The Reference Librarian* 69/70 (2000): 363–78.

Rutgers. "Library Terminology: A Guide for International Students." http://www.libraries.rutgers.edu/rul/lib_servs/intl_students_terms.shtml (accessed October 20, 2010).

Zhang, Li. "Communication in Academic Libraries: An East Asian Perspective." *Reference Services Review* 34, no. 1 (2006): 164–76.

4 LIVE ONLINE—CHAT, PUSH, AND COBROWSING

CHAT

Chat will look familiar to some of us over 30. It's pretty much the old Internet relay chat from the 1990s but more usable now with faster PCs and handheld devices. Many of the abbreviations are the same, such as LOL (lots of laughs) and BTW (by the way). Many are new; if you search for chat slang, there are a number of lists available (Crystal 2004). You may need them to translate your patron's jargon, but don't use them in your responses unless you actually know the patron and know that he will understand them.

Chat is an interactive service that has all the possibilities of a face-to-face reference interview. Patrons usually choose chat because it's perceived as a faster method, but that's not necessarily true. It generally takes longer than picking up the phone and calling since speech is usually faster than typing. Chat does meet patron's desire for a familiar and anonymous media. It also meets the patron's need for a service that goes wherever he does—if he has a laptop or a cell phone. It also has no travel time, a large consideration for many patrons.

The downside of that need for speed is that patrons want their information with the speed of Google, and librarians are real flesh-and-blood people. In our jargon, Google is ready reference, but we are the real search engines. We can find the information they haven't been able to, but it will take some time.

Like other services, you'll want to tell the patrons before they begin that answers may take time, that they may have to wait until the next day for the answer, and that they may have to answer more questions to get the information they need. Put it in obvious place near your contact information. Some patrons will still miss it, but it can give your patrons a more realistic view of what they can expect.

How people feel about the library and the reference transaction affects their learning. If they hate the library and feel frustrated by the librarian, they will go back to Google. If they feel that the librarian is interested in them and helpful, they will stay through the process and come back again. Recognizing and acknowledging the patron's feelings, whatever they are, makes the patron feel that he has a legitimate question and is working with a helpful and caring person, even if the results are not what he expected or wanted. The librarian is a coach, helping the patron both to find what he wants and to learn to find it on his own.

Many of your online patrons will be young. More older patrons come online every day, but younger ones sometimes seem to be born online. More than 80 percent of teens use instant messaging or chat services for other purposes (Valenza 2003). That also means that they are used to instant answers, but you can be sure that patrons have already checked Google before they ask your service. Google is the first step in research for anyone, of any age, who has a computer.

Since there are no nonverbal clues in chat or any other online service, the open question is critical. If 70 percent of interpersonal communication comes from body language, you are left with only 30 percent to work with (Fernandez 2004). Without input from the patron, the interview becomes a monologue and not a dialogue. The librarian can construct the question and answer it, too. That doesn't help the patron at all.

If the patron asks about "women and politics" in his initial question, the librarian could take that information and start feeding him information about current female political figures when he might have wanted statistical information about women's voting patterns or suffragettes in England. Most people are too polite to interrupt and say that you have it wrong. They may wait and then say "what I *really* need is . . . " something totally different. Both of you have lost time that could have been avoided using the same practices you use in face-to-face interviews.

In addition, you have lost the patron's trust that you are really a knowledgeable and helpful person since you responded to the surface question, not unlike Google would. Patrons seldom come to you before trying search engines, so while you think you've done a good job, the patron thinks you are another software application. The way that you distinguish yourself from software and search engines isn't how you answer or even what you answer; rather. it's what and how you ask.

The online environment doesn't give you many clues to what the patron needs, so you need to ask often and clarify even more often. You are a more sophisticated and experienced searcher, but you need to be a better questioner. Time is often a perceived pressure online, but you always have time to ask another question that will help you both. If you feel pressured or hate keying, write some scripted questions similar to what you say at the desk. Have the encouragers, too. By now you know how effective they are, so be sure to use them online, too.

Patrons give and take information in chunks. The farther the interview goes, the larger the chunks tend to be as you figure out what the patron really needs. Be aware that there is a limit to how much someone can take in and use at one sitting. It's rare that the patron will retain much of what you say if you say too much. Yes, you know all about finding information, but the patron cares only about his need, and when he has enough, he will stop you. He might say, "That's good" or "Okay, I've got it"; he may just log off. It is hoped that you will catch his clues before you get to that point, but it will happen, even in short interviews (Libutti and Tipton 2004).

Make sure that your link site explains the limitations of your service, such as serving a limited area (our patrons only; enter you library card number now), having limited sources, and having a limited time frame (not instant like Google). Also explain the advantages, such as providing expert help, having more sources than Google, and having a real person at the other end (that's not obvious to patrons). You want your patrons to know all this before they log on to save your time and theirs.

You also want to start with as much information as you can. It's good to have a Web form that will give you the question when you start the chat instead of starting form scratch, especially since many patrons will log on even if they're not part of your service group. It can save you a lot of keying, too. You'll still have to use the reference interview to get to the real question, so save keystrokes when you can.

Your search time and typing time is dead air for the patron, who is used to getting responses in seconds from Google. Keep telling them what you're doing. You might even keep a list of responses to tell them that you're "still working," but don't let your responses sound too canned. Have several messages for the same thing, such as "I'm looking at sources now," "I'm still looking," and "Sorry it's taking so long, but I'm still looking." That will keep you sounding like a human and not a voice-mail menu.

You can use scripts for greetings or inappropriate questions or comments, explaining a particular database or that a patron isn't eligible to use your service. You'll undoubtedly find other phrases that are useful, too. You might have longer ones for technical problems with library resources or keep URLs for help sites handy. If you tend to use jargon, have explanations scripted so that you don't stop the transaction in its tracks. Or, better yet, use simpler terms. Remember, jargon is our language, not theirs.

Use emoticons as little as possible. Smiley faces in your introduction are friendly; beyond that, they get cluttered, and you risk confusing patrons who don't know what they mean. If patrons use emoticons, you can be a little freer with them. Chat and other online communication are not sophisticated and nuanced, and emoticons don't make them any more so.

On the other hand, emoticons can make the interview a little friendlier, so it may depend on your context. Do you work for an academic library or a public one? Patrons will have different expectations for each of them, and your boss may have still other ideas for their use.

Although chat is casual, you may want to keep a more formal tone than that of your patrons. You are the voice of authority in the information science sense. You don't want to come across as one in the social sense, though; you want to be friendly but efficient. In terms of Ranganathan's laws, you are saving the time of the user, and you do that by being effective.

Chat is anonymous. It's like the famous 1993 *New Yorker* cartoon: "On the Internet, no one knows you're a dog." You may be chatting with a professor or instant messaging with a 10-year-old, and you may never know. That's a good thing. You can give equal service on a level that isn't influenced by appearances, age, or any other factor except need. The bad part is that you won't know, unless the patron tells you or you ask, what level of information the patron needs.

Don't let your keyboarding skills get in the way of your service. Typos happen; everyone has misspellings. It doesn't make you look dumb unless you have a spell-checker that changes the word wrong: "garage" and "garbage," "trail" and "trial," everyone had experienced it. You can correct it or apologize if you must, but unless it's creating a problem in giving the answer, you're wasting the patron's time. If you feel compelled to apologize, put a line in your scripts: you don't want to mistype your apology, too.

Recent research show that patrons don't care about misspellings (Hansen et al. 2009). They seldom correct misspellings in casual texting, so they are used to them. You need to correct only names and words that are important to finding the information they need. Speed and convenience are more important factors than spelling.

In theory, you can do online reference from anywhere you have access to the resources. Most of us don't have the paper copies at home to look up anything that's not online, but if your patrons don't use the *Oxford English Dictionary* or encyclopedias, it's possible. If you have the right subscription databases, you can do that, too. It's definitely possible to do it from you office, and there'll be fewer distractions. It will take longer to look up answers in paper sources, but it's still faster than fielding in-person questions while you try to find the answer for an online patron.

Some—perhaps many—of your sessions will start from within the library. With the popularity of handheld devices and Wi-Fi, you can literally be at the patron's point of need, with neither of you traveling to where the other is, even if that's just a floor away. Don't think like an old person—that he's being lazy by not coming to you in person. Rather, he's being polite by not insisting that you come to him. Synchronous reference means that you can be at his point of need, not just physically but also temporally.

Your chat software may allow cobrowsing, where the patron can see your screen and interact with it, too, or page pushing, where you can send a page to the patron. That will allow you to show the patron exactly what you're doing and talking about and let him have some control over the resources while you chat. It's the equivalent of turning your monitor to the patron in a face-to-face interview.

If you can cobrowse or push a page to patrons, warn them before you start. It's startling to have a page suddenly appear, and they may close the window to look for their reference chat again. If you can't cobrowse in your software, you can always ask them to open the site you want them to look at and chat as you look in parallel (Ronan 2007).

Explain what you're doing as you work. Seeing without explanation isn't very helpful, as you need to keep the conversation going.

INSTANT MESSAGING

Instant messaging is another old technology that has found a new life. Instant messages usually pop up on your screen, and you can answer directly from the box. They are good for short exchanges, but you may want a more sophisticated interface for more sophisticated questions. Instant messaging removes some of the distractions found in the face-to-face interview. There are no ringing phones on your end, and there is no line to wait in on his (Ruppel and Fagan 2002).

Instant messaging requires active involvement of patrons. They can't just listen; rather, they have to type and respond. Of course, if they're not interested or if they don't think you're helping, they can just hit the exit button instead of walking away. Or they may lose the connection and leave involuntarily, and you may never know which. Delays may mean that your users are done, that they're looking at their assignment, or maybe that they're just slow typists.

If you have the patron's name from the log-in or it appears on-screen, use it in your greeting instead of your canned greeting. Use a name, too. It doesn't have to be your real name; you can let each librarian pick one or be "Dick" and "Jane." But names add a personal touch that's missing in remote services. A name also lets you trace who answered the question in case the patron needs more help.

Keep comments short. You don't have to be Twitter short, but reading long text blocks is hard online, and they'll slow the pace of the interview. If the patron has a cell phone interface, it may not even fit on the display screen. Make them a sentence long, not a paragraph long.

It's also hard to know when one person is done "talking." If you keep messages short, you won't "talk over" your patron's responses. If you're out of sync, both of you may become confused about who is talking about what.

Avoid questions that have yes/no answers. They do save keying time, but they can come across as unfriendly or rude. They also don't advance your interview, so save them for when you know that those are the only alternatives.

Avoid jargon unless you have a scripted explanation of it (American Library Association 2005). You can spend a lot of time explaining what you just said when you could have just said it more simply. That doesn't mean that your patron won't use his own jargon; people have used their own jargon online for many years. Emoticons go back to the late 1970s and ARPANET, but they have new variants. If your patrons think you're not understanding them, they'll often switch to standard spelling and punctuation. You should be that polite as well.

You'll run into rude patrons online, too. Use the same techniques you use with face-to-face patrons. Don't fall into the trap of reflecting their behavior. Don't scold them for being rude, as you'll just escalate things.

COLLABORATIVE REFERENCE

Collaborative reference can be as simple as a phone system that forwards calls to another library when you're closed or as complicated as an online system that covers an entire country. Online systems may queue questions for the next available librarian or direct them to a library that is online at the moment or that has special resources. While such systems are collaborations between libraries and systems, they don't allow several librarians to work on the same question at the same time within the system. What they do well is allow a patron to ask a question when it's on his mind.

Some online services aggregate many libraries to cover the times and subjects that one library can't on its own. A question submitted from a rural public library can be routed to a university with a subject specialist. A question that can be answered only from primary sources can be answered by the archive that holds them.

There are definite advantages but some disadvantages, too. With a central point for answering, patrons don't know who they're asking. That can lead to problems. Many reference questions online are just like they are in person: questions about local services, such as fines and circulation. If you're from another library, you can't access their records to answer the question and will have to refer them back to their home library. Because of contract terms, you can't use the databases that you have access to for questions outside your patron base. In larger collaborations, the library you need to refer the patron to is in another time zone and is closed

You won't be able to answer questions about local services and local interest questions. You'll have to search the other library's website for policies and procedures or copy them to your frequently-asked-questions site and hope they don't change. You won't have the resources to look up phone numbers for a school or city directories to check old addresses. Your patron will be surprised that you don't have these resources, so have a scripted reply explaining that he didn't really reach his local library. You'll use it a lot.

You'll also get a lot of questions referred to you from other libraries that have picked up questions they can't answer. Be prepared for some confusion from all parties involved. You'll have less if you make it clear on your website that the service covers a large area and that your library isn't necessarily the one they will reach. That doesn't mean that you won't get those questions since this is a very convenient way to ask questions, but you want to not confuse or dissatisfy more patrons than you need to.

Collaborative reference certainly will advance in the future, just as collaborative cataloging has. Possibilities include blogs, where librarians can contribute, and wikis (Pomerantz and Stutzman 2006). Open-source software can make collaborative services economically viable. Answers can be captured in searchable databases for later use. That will make life online much easier for the librarian, but it will still be limited to information that has been found. Information that isn't cataloged or indexed will still need a librarian's hand.

Some of these services are already available but not yet in a combination that meets all libraries' needs, let alone all patrons. Nor is there any guarantee that Web 2.0 services are sustainable over a long period of time. If funding fails or an organization ceases to exist, who will archive all those answers? How will they be preserved if the world moves to another system? Those are questions that apply to all free online services. Sooner or later—and preferably sooner—we will have to find answers.

REFERENCES

American Library Association. "RUSA Guidelines for Behavioral Performance of Reference and Information Service Providers." August 5, 2005. http://www.ala.org/ala/rusa/rusaprotools/referenceguide/guidelinesbehavioral.htm (accessed October 11, 2010).

Crystal, D. *A Glossary of Netspeak and Textspeak*. Edinburgh: Edinburgh University Press, 2004.

Fernandez, J. "Facing Live Reference." *Online: The Leading Magazine for Information Professionals* 28, no. 3 (2004): 37–40.

Hansen, Derek, Margeaux Johnson, Elizabeth Norton, and Anne McDonough. "Virtual Provider Pessimism: Analysing Instant Messaging Reference Encounters with the Pair Perception Comparison Method." *Information Research* 14, no. 1 (March 2009). http://informationr.net/ir/14-4/paper416.html (accessed July 21, 2010).

Libutti, Patricia O'Brien, and Roberta Tipton. *Digital Resources and Librarians: Case Studies in Innovation, Invention, and Implementation*. Chicago: American Library Association, 2004.

Pomerantz, Jeffrey, and Frederic Stutzman. "Collaborative Reference Work in the Blogosphere." *Reference Service Review* 34, no. 2 (2006): 200–213.

Ronan, Jana Smith. *Chat and the Reference Interview Online*. Westport, CT: Libraries Unlimited, 2007.

Ruppel, Margie, and Jody Condit Fagan. "Instant Messaging Reference: Users' Evaluation of Library Chat." *Reference Services Review* 30, no. 3 (2002): 183–97.

Valenza, J. K. "IMing Means Never Having to Say You're Not There." *Voice of Youth Advocates* 26, no. 4 (2003): 291.

FURTHER READING

Acronymfinder. http://www.acronymfinder.com (accessed October 20, 2010). Searchable database of more than 2,445,000 abbreviations and acronyms.

Bobrowsky, T., L. Beck, and M. Grant. "The Chat Reference Interview: Practicalities and Advice." *The Reference Librarian* 43, no. 89 (2005): 179–91.

Bowman, V. "The Virtual Librarian and the Electronic Reference Interview." *Internet Reference Services Quarterly* 7, no. 3 (2002): 3–14.

Bridgewater, Rachel, and Meryl B. Cole. *Instant Messaging Reference: A Practical Guide*. Oxford: Chandos Publishing, 2008.

Carter, D. S. "Hurry Up and Wait: Observations and Tips about the Practice of Chat Reference." *The Reference Librarian* 79/80 (2002/2003): 113–20.

Chase, Darren. "Papa's Got a Brand New (Virtual) Bag: Real-Time Chat and Reference Discourse." *Electronic Journal of Academic and Special Librarianship* 6, no. 1–2 (Summer 2005). http://southernlibrarianship.icaap.org/content/v06n01/chase_d01.htm (accessed August 20, 2010).

Coffman, Steve. *Going Live: Starting and Running a Virtual Reference Service*. Chicago: American Library Association, 2003.

Coffman, Steve. "What's Wrong with Collaborative Digital Reference?" *American Libraries* 33, no. 11 (December 2002): 56–58.

Crystal, D. *Language and the Internet*. Cambridge: Cambridge University Press, 2001.

Curry, E. L. "The Reference Interview Revisited: Librarian-Patron Interaction in the Virtual Environment." *Simile* 5, no. 1 (February 2005): 1–16.

Desai, C. M. "Instant Message Reference: How Does It Compare?" *The Electronic Library* 21, no. 1 (2003): 21–30.

Doherty, J. J. "Reference Interview or Reference Dialogue?" *Internet Reference Services Quarterly* 11, no. 3 (2006): 95–107.

Fagan, J. C., and C. M. Desai. "Communication Strategies for Instant Messaging and Chat Reference Services." *The Reference Librarian* 79/80 (2002/2003): 121–55.

Houghton, S., and A. Schmidt. "Web-Based Chat vs. Instant Messaging: Who Wins?" *Online* 29, no. 4 (2005): 26–30.

Hvass, A., and S. Myer. "Can I Help You? Implementing an IM Service." *Electronic Library* 26, no. 4 (2008): 530–44.

International Federation of Library Associations. "IFLA Digital Reference Guidelines." http://archive.ifla.org/VII/s36/pubs/drg03.htm#2.1 (accessed October 15, 2010).

Janes, J. "Follow Their Lead, Dawg." *American Libraries* 35, no. 10 (2004): 56.

Janes, J., and J. Silverstein. "Question Negotiation and the Technological Environment." *D-Lib Magazine* 9, no. 2 (2003). http://www.dlib.org/dlib/february03/janes/02janes.html (accessed July 20, 2010).

Jennerich, Edward. *Reference Interview in the Digital Age*. Westport, CT: Libraries Unlimited, 2003.

Katz, B., ed. *Digital Reference Services*. Hawthorne, NJ: Hawthorne Information Press, 2003.

Kazmer, Michelle, Gary Burnett, and Michael Dickey. "Identity in Customer Service Chat Interaction: Implications for Virtual Reference." *Library and Information Science Research* 29, no. 1 (2007): 26.

Kimmel, S., and J. Heise. *Virtual Reference Services: Issues and Trends*. Hawthorne, NJ: Hawthorne Information Press, 2003.

Kluegel, K. "The Reference Interview through Time and Space." *Reference and User Services Quarterly* 43, no. 1 (2003): 37.

Kovacs, Diane Kaye. *The Virtual Reference Handbook: Interview and Information Delivery Techniques for the Chat and E-Mail Environments*. New York: Neal-Schuman, 2007.

Kwon, N., and V. Gregory. "The Effects of Librarians' Behavioral Performance on User Satisfaction in Chat Reference Services." *Reference & User Services Quarterly* 47, no. 2 (2006): 137–48.

Lipow, Anne Grodzins. *The Virtual Reference Librarian's Handbook*. New York: Neal-Schuman, 2003.

Luo, Lili. "Toward Sustaining Professional Development: Identifying Essential Competencies for Chat Reference Service." *Library & Information Science Research* 30, no. 4 (2008): 298–311.

Marsteller, M. R., and D. Mizzy. "Exploring the Synchronous Digital Reference Interaction for Query Types, Question Negotiation, and Patron Response." *Internet Reference Services Quarterly* 8, no. 1–2 (2003): 149–65.

Meola, Marc, and Sam Stormant. *Starting and Operating Live Virtual Reference Services: A How to Do It Manual for Librarians*. New York: Neal-Schuman, 2002.

Mon, L., E. G. Abels, D. E. Agosto, et al. "Remote Reference in U.S. Public Library Practice and LIS Education." *Journal of Education for Library and Information Science* 49 (2008): 180–94.

Net Lingo. http://www.netlingo.com (accessed October 21, 2010). Dictionary of Internet terms, symbols, and abbreviations.

Nilsen, K. "Virtual versus Face-to-Face Reference: Comparing Users' Perspectives on Visits to Physical and Virtual Reference Desks in Public and Academic Libraries." In: Proceedings of Libraries: A Voyage of Discovery, 2005.

Ovadia, S. "Real-Time Chat Reference and the Importance of Text-Chat." *The Reference Librarian* 79/80 (2002/2003): 157–61.

QuestionPoint. "QuestionPoint Reference Management Service Provides Libraries with Web-Based Tools to Interact with Users Using Both Chat and Email." http://www .oclc.org/questionpoint/default.htm (accessed July 14, 2010).

Resnick, Taryn Ana Ugaz, and Nancy Burford. "E-resource Helpdesk into Virtual Reference: Identifying Core Competencies." *Reference Services Review* 38, no. 3 (2010): 347–59.

Ronan, Janna. *Chat Reference: A Guide to Live Virtual Reference Services*. Westport, CT: Libraries Unlimited, 2003.

Ronan, Jana, Patrick Reakes, and Marilyn Ochoa. "Application of Reference Guidelines in Chat Reference Interactions: A Study of Online Reference Skills." *College and Undergraduate Libraries* 13, no. 4 (2006): 3–30.

Shachaf, P., and S. Horowitz. "Are Virtual Reference Services Color Blind?" *Library & Information Science Research* 28, no. 4 (2007): 501–20.

Shachaf, Pnina, and Mary Snyder. "The Relationship between Cultural Diversity and User Needs in Virtual Reference Services." *Journal of Academic Librarianship* 33, no. 3 (2007): 361–67.

Shucha, Bonnie. "IM a Librarian: Establishing a Virtual Reference Service with Little Cost or Technical Skill." August 27, 2007. http://www.llrx.com/features/virtualreference service.htm (accessed October 14, 2010).

Silverstein, Joanne. "Just Curious: Children's Use of Digital Reference for Unimposed Queries and Its Importance in Informal Education." *Library Trends* 54, no. 2 (Fall 2005): 228–44.

Straw, J. "A Virtual Understanding: The Reference Interview and Question Negotiation in a Digital Age." *Reference and User Services Quarterly* 39, no. 4 (Summer 2000): 376–79.

Taher, M. "Real-Time (Synchronous Interactive) Reference Interview: A Select Bibliography." *Internet Reference Services Quarterly* 7, no. 3 (2002): 35–41.

Tenopir, C. "Chat's Positive Side." *Library Journal* 129, no. 20 (2004): 42.

Wikoff, N. "Reference Transaction Handoffs: Factors Affecting the Transition from Chat to E-mail." *Reference and User Services Quarterly* 47, no. 3 (2008): 230–41.

5 SHORT BURSTS—TWEETS, TEXT, AND THE NEXT BIG THING

Much has been written about the Millennial generation. Millennials haven't read it. Millennials don't read a great deal that's not online. The Web is their information universe, and Google is their librarian. They communicate by text, by Twitter, and by means not even invented as I write this. They know that they can get information instantly. Few of them know whether that information is reliable, and many of them don't care. When they research, good enough is enough.

That's a big change in attitude for many of us. It's part of our job to teach them how to sort the wheat from the chaff, a phrase that means nothing if you didn't grow up on a wheat farm. Information literacy is essential for anyone in the digital age. You can teach them as you search, you can teach them in information literacy classes, but the real teaching opportunity is when they actually need the information. The problem is catching them at that point.

Patrons are no longer anchored by a computer; they can reach people and services by their phones. Can they reach you? Are you invisible to them? To use your services via a mobile application, you will need to optimize your pages to work with a smaller screen. Some vendors offer mobile versions, so you won't need to recode everything.

Of course, we are not limited to what our phones can do. Many services can be sent or received at your computer, not your phone. That's less expensive and easier on the hands than a phone keypad.

There are several ways to run a short message service (SMS) reference service, from for-pay software to simply buying a phone and service. Cost and ease of use are two big factors in making a choice; if the librarian is frustrated by the technical aspects, he will not be as friendly as he might be. Give the librarians who aren't used to texting a chance to practice with the phone. A full keyboard will be easier to learn than a numerical keypad, but it still takes practice. This is one new media that requires you to learn and practice new physical skills, so make sure you are comfortable with it before you answer questions on it.

If you have sufficient information technology skills or someone in the library does, you can patch together a number of freeware applications to customize your own service. That may include transferring the message to an instant messaging or e-mail service. Then you can use a regular keyboard and concentrate on the interview instead of your thumbs. Then you have to keep track of only how many characters you've typed, but there will be freeware for that a soon as the need is recognized.

TEXTING

We know that teens and twenties text a lot. Their cell phones are the center of their lives in many ways and certainly the center of their communications. We know that people will text from within the library, so why don't we take advantage of the methods they already use (Pearce, Collard, and Whatley 2010)? SMS isn't a particularly good medium for asking or answering questions, but it does have its uses in the reference setting. If patrons are using it, why aren't we?

You might have to learn still another language. The older acronyms like BTW (by the way) are still used, but there are many more needed to communicate in a few characters. Some are fairly obvious, if you think about them, such as B4 (before). Others will take a dictionary (or a teen) to decipher. Don't be too discouraged; if you move to a chat or an e-mail interface, they really can speak and write standard English for us old people. Old people are generically those of use over 30, no matter how cool we are. Text abbreviations are, in principle, the same as any slang you used in your youth. It didn't prevent you from completing college—it just made it easier to talk to friends.

SMS is good for ready-reference and quick factual questions, which are actually drawn-out questions if you have to go to the library to ask. Hours, services, and factual questions are easy to answer in 140 characters. The relationship between mental illness and creativity will take a lot more time and space. That's a case where you want to say yes, we have resources, what's your e-mail, and I'll send you the citations.

SMS may turn librarians into human search engines, a role already taken by Cha-Cha and KGB, although those are for-fee services. It's not necessarily a bad thing, except that librarians are in short supply and can seldom afford the time to monitor several SMS accounts. That may be a job for paraprofessionals who can refer more complicated questions to a librarian to answer via e-mail or chat. Some SMS widgets aggregate accounts from different software into a single account, which is much easier to monitor and manage.

One advantage of a texting service is that you can do it very cheaply, so you won't have a great deal invested if no one uses it or something new comes along (Boeninger 2010). You can combine a number of free services and software to meet your needs and then proceed to help your patrons.

The short nature of SMS makes the reference interview sound like a game of 20 questions to patrons, and they may feel like they aren't getting an answer. It also makes it very easy for an anonymous user to simply disconnect in that case. Don't let the disconnects get you down, though. Sometimes the patron leaves to think about what you've said and will be back later.

TWITTER

Twitter is the best-known SMS service at the moment. Whether it will last doesn't matter because it will certainly be replaced by another service that lets people communicate quickly from anywhere. It's too convenient not to live on in some guise.

Twitter is a typical SMS service in that messages are limited in length to 140 characters. That's not much for reference questions, although it works for directional and ready-reference questions. The best reference use for SMS may be to use it as a broadcast to publicize services you offer. The British Library is using it that way but as of November 2010 had only 19 followers. The British Library is not a destination for younger patrons, so it may not be the best comparison. If you repurpose posts from another source, that may be good enough. If you have to rewrite them to shorten them, it may not be worth the effort. If it costs you nothing but time, give it a try. Your library may be overrun with tweeters that you never knew about. Put your tag on a quick-response (QR) code sticker and give them out or post it where your younger patrons are.

Twitter is flexible. You can send and receive messages from your phone or a computer where they will be shown on a Web page or as instant messages. That gives your patrons some choice of how they get the information and gives you some in how you send it. Still, you're limited in the message length. You may want to use it to publicize your text and e-mail reference services rather than answer the questions themselves.

There are also privacy issues on Twitter since the comments are posted on the website. That might make it a good choice for ready-reference and directional questions but a bad one for confidential issues. Most die-hard Tweeters know that, but new users can be surprised to find their information online. That may not be an issue now, but there are many "Twitter quitters" who forget that they ever had an account and will not be happy to find their information online in years hence.

SMS must often move to another medium for longer answers. Some people will follow a long answer in several parts, but many people will broadcast their question to everyone they know and get answers before a librarian can give them a reliable one. They want instant information, and who can blame them in an age when Google Wave came and went in less than a year's time? Software, as well as service, moves at a modern pace. If you use Twitter for reference, post some message that will assure them it still exists at least daily but not more than six or seven times a day. If you stop using Twitter, send out a message announcing it so that you don't alienate your followers.

If you send an answer in several parts, make sure it's easy for the patron to find those parts. Make sure you can find them, too. It's easy to get lost if you're dealing with several questions at once or a repeat user who's coming back for more information assumes that you remember him. Twitter is a conversational medium, so it may work for the reference interview, but it will work only for short answers.

When you send a URL, you can shorten it with services like bit.ly or tiny.url. That not only gives you fewer characters to send but also makes a long URL shorter, meaning that it won't wrap in an e-mail, either. That saves the patron from cutting and pasting, with potentially an added space and an incorrect URL.

Twitter is a good medium for telling people that you're friendly and helpful and that you can be reached other ways. Be sure to give them those ways; a phone number, a URL, or an e-mail address invites them to continue the conversation as a reference interview.

QR CODES

QR codes are the square tags that look like scrambled bar codes. You can read them with an application on your cell phone or anything else that will let you scan. They're fairly new but already much used in retail, so your patrons have probably seen more than you have. QR codes are the answer to the perennial problem of remembering a URL or trying to type it in. With a cell phone, you can send it to your e-mail account or view it on your phone.

QR codes can do a lot of things. They can do mundane things, like bar codes can, but they can do much more. They can give you URLs that contain more information about an item, animations, or anything that you want. Since QR codes lead you to other information, they are like Web surfing, but the information they lead to is controlled by you.

You can provide point-of-use instruction at point-of-need locations. Think of QR codes on your public computers that lead to instructions for the databases. They can lead to software tutorials. They can lead to information literacy tutorials. You can link to a podcast from a poster. You can put the QR code on a keychain or a bookmark. Think about a tote bag that has two uses: carrying books and publicizing your library's reference services.

You can link to read-alikes from a book spine or to reviews of the book from publications or by patrons. You can send patrons to the reference desk for help or give them the reference desk phone number or directions and hours. QR codes in the stacks could bring up a list of LibGuides on topics related to books in the call number range.

You can direct users to a service that's specifically aimed at mobile device users, such as a chat or instant messaging reference service or the mobile version of the library's catalog or databases. Remember that you have to optimize the sites for cell phones in that case. As more and more people use cell phones for Web access, more vendors are providing that already. WorldCat Mobile is a good example.

6 ASYNCHRONOUS REFERENCE

You might think that asynchronous reference is dead in the age of Twitter, e-mail, and the ubiquitous cell phone. You would be wrong. The digital divide still exists, in the United States as well as much of the rest of the world. There are people who don't have computers, who don't have a local library connection, and who can't afford cell phones. There are people who don't use them because of a disability. There are also people who just don't like them. If you can't answer a question immediately and have to get back to the patron, it becomes asynchronous.

It's difficult to go from one method to another any time; following up by an older method is more reliable and as quick in many cases. You need to have a way to connect the parts of phone, fax, or e-mail to each other or to another service. Unless you can guarantee that you will take the next call or get the fax, it's no different than turning your back on the patron. You can use a folder for e-mails or faxes and make sure the patron has your cell number (if you have one for work) or some other method to contact you. It will also be useful if you need to pass the transaction off to another librarian in your library or somewhere else as a referral.

There are advantages to asynchronous service. The patron doesn't expect an instant answer, so you have time to search. Neither of you has to be a speed typist, so you have time to think about your responses. You don't have to know what ROTFL 2F! means. You have more options to offer in giving the patron your response: mail, fax, as an attachment to an e-mail, or a an FTP file. You don't have a line of patrons tapping their feet, and a ringing phone can be answered without apology. But it is slower from both sides.

MAIL

Most of your mail questions will come from patrons who are not in a hurry and who live at some distance. They tend to be genealogists and serious researchers, whether academic or not, who can't find the information locally. Your policies will determine whether you refer them to a local source or answer their questions. It is more common for archives to get inquiries by mail and to answer them that way since they will be the only place that has the information. Some of their requests can be answered by referring them to interlibrary loan at their local library, but in some cases they may be trying to get around that process because of restrictions at one end or the other.

The good part of mail questions is that if patrons take the time to write and mail their question, they usually include all the information they have and where they have already looked. They may include how they found you and who referred them and be very specific about what they want. The bad side is that if they didn't give you any background, it may take weeks or months to complete the interview by exchanging a series of letters. You'll want to ask for a phone or e-mail address in your initial reply and ask for any other information explicitly.

Some of these patrons write because they don't have access or simply don't like faster technologies, so be prepared to keep a paper folder for each correspondent's mail so that you can track where you stand in the process.

People who write are generally more formal than those that e-mail, so make your answers a little more formal than you would for e-mail. Be sure to have your contact information and that of the library in your reply since inquiry letters are often sent to many libraries and archives. You want to make sure they know who the information is coming from and how to get back to you again.

Since the patron may assume that he sent you all the information that you need, explain why you need more to answer his question. In archives, which are often contacted by mail, the patron may not realize that archives are not organized like libraries and that huge amounts of information may exist that the archivist cannot research for each patron. Many archives keep lists of independent researchers and students who can be hired to do the research for them if the patron's question is too broad to be answered with the tools available locally.

Questions by mail may also assume that you will send the answer that way, even if it's hundreds of pages. If you have limits to what you will do for patrons or what you can send, it's a good idea to have them on the website with your physical address. Just like from your end of the interview, the more information you have at the start, the better the interview. If you don't have that information online, include that information in your initial response.

Patrons will often send a self-addressed stamped envelope, saving you both postage and from having to decipher their handwriting. You can request one in your online instructions, but be prepared for the patron to ask for more information than will fit in a small envelope. People who write tend to be traditionalists and want a paper copies of everything you have.

PHONE

Phone reference is another favorite of patrons who don't use high-tech services. It has the advantages of being immediate, easy to use, and personal. Like other distance reference services, is has the disadvantages of not letting you or the patron see any nonverbal cues. Phone is a common venue for ready-reference questions and short factual questions, but other questions will require all your skills.

Phone calls are usually lower in your priorities than face-to-face interviews. They may go to answering machines or voice mail, or you may have time to answer and take a number to return the call. If you have voice mail, make the menu short. People call the library to talk to a person and may not wait for a long menu to finish.

Be sure of your library's policy regarding phone reference. Is it limited to ready-reference questions? Is it limited by time? Is it limited to your local patrons or available to others? Can you answer homework questions or contest questions? Is there an answering machine if you can't take a call? If not, patrons will stop calling you. How often should you check it? Whose responsibility is it? Since phone is one of the oldest methods of long-distance reference, you should already have a policy, but it should be reviewed often enough to make it useful.

When answering the phone, identify yourself and your library. This is your greeting, and, just like in-person service, you want it to be welcoming and warm. Try recording yourself and listening to it. Your voice doesn't sound the same to you as it does to other people. You will be surprised at what you really sound like, so take the chance to rehearse your greeting and get it right. You can rehearse your answering skills and hear what you sound like to your patrons. Do you hesitate? Do you use a lot of "uhh . . . " to fill in spaces? Don't talk too fast, as that can sound curt and make you difficult to understand. "Too fast" will depend on where you are: normal to a Michigander will sound fast to an Alabaman but slow to a New Yorker.

Answer with a smile—it'll show in your voice. Always give the patron a confirmation that they've reached the right place. "Hello, this is Katie at the Big Library reference desk." Then, if you get cut off, they know who to ask for or who to refer to if they call back another time. Besides, it's just polite.

If the patron mentions his name during the interview, try to use it in the conversation. That can give it a personal touch that's lacking when you're not face-to-face. Try to jot it down so that you'll remember it when you get a chance. Don't be too surprised if the patron corrects you, asks you to use his title ("I'm Doctor Smith"), or rebuffs you. Apologize and keep going. Some people will find it pushy even though they've given you their name.

The reference interview will consist of the usual questions unless the patron needs the materials sent or you need to return the call later. If you have to leave the phone to find the answer or put it down to use the computer, tell the patron. Otherwise, it sounds like you've simply fallen asleep. Time is distorted while you're waiting; two minutes can seem like an hour. If you'll be more than two minutes, go back and give the patron the option of your returning the call when you have found the answer or holding while you search. Putting a patron on hold is preferable to just putting the phone down since it eliminates the patron having to listen to chatter at the desk or people picking the phone up to see if someone's there. Explain to the patron so that he doesn't think that the connection has been lost.

Very often the patron will ask you to call back rather than wait. Your reference has just become asynchronous, so be prepared to shift modes mentally, too. A new twist in the cellular world is asking the patron if it's a good time to talk when you return calls. After all, they may be anywhere, and while driving is not a good time to write down citation information.

If you need to transfer a call to another librarian or department, explain that to the patron and give him the name and number in case the call doesn't go through. Tell the person you're calling all the information you have thus far, and you'll save time for both parties. If the person whom the patron needs to talk to isn't there, give the patron the hours he can be reached.

With phone systems becoming more complicated, have the instructions for forwarding a call next to the phone or taped to it. If you don't do it often, you'll forget. If you forget, you may lose the call instead of transferring it.

When you give the answer, make sure the patron has pencil and paper first so that he can write it down. Ask if he's ready for you to read the answer. Give the source you're using and the date. Spell any words that might be misheard, names, and technical terms. Talk slowly enough that he can take notes and ask if he'd like you to repeat any of it. You can also give the option of sending a long answer by mail or e-mail. If you offer to send it by postal mail, be sure to cover the details of who pays for the postage and get a complete address.

If you can't answer a question immediately, be sure to set up a way to get back in touch with the patron. Repeat the information back so that you know it's right. If an answer will take a while, make sure to get at least one way to get back with him, be that by phone, e-mail, fax, or all of these. Tell him when to expect you—at least a range, such as 10 minutes, two hours, or tomorrow—and ask if that works for him. If it doesn't, give him the contact information for another institution or invite him to come to the library in person.

If you're passing the question to another shift or librarian, get all the information to contact the patron and list what you've done already. A form can help you keep track of what you've done and for whom. Be sure to leave lots of room for your notes; you'll be saving the next librarian's time if you pass along everything and everywhere you've already looked. Print it on colored paper so that it won't get lost in the shuffle of papers that happens at desks or flipped and used for scratch paper. You can cut down some on your writing if you have check boxes for commonly used sources or the amount of information needed:

- Patron's name
- Preferred phone number and time to call
- Affiliation (are they in your service area or group?)
- Subject of research: the basic question plus anything you found out in the interview
- Purpose of the research
- Deadline
- Type and amount of information needed: data? dates? articles?
- Names of people being researched

- Where they lived
- What they did
- What time period covered: modern? historical? last week?
- What sources you have checked already
- Notes
- Sources consulted
- Time and date of the call
- Date answer given
- Your name

If names are confusing, spell them out phonetically as well in your notes (Ohio Reference Excellence 2008). You may need to check variant spellings in your research or to pronounce them correctly when returning a call.

E-MAIL

If your patron is asking the same question at a dozen different places, it's much more efficient for him to write one e-mail and send it everywhere than make a dozen calls. That's often the case for genealogists and other researchers who are willing to give you what they already know and ask you what is available at your library. It's often the case for younger students, who will write everywhere and hope to get enough information for an assignment but will give you little background to work with.

Getting that information is what takes time, something patrons don't expect from e-mail. If the question takes research, reply immediately and let him know what time frame to expect an answer in, just like you do in returning phone calls. You can have an automated acknowledgment reply that goes to patrons who e-mail the reference desk, too. You want the patron to know you're there and that you got his e-mail. If you have a time frame to answer it, include that, too. If there are websites that have related information, you might send them for him to read while waiting for your response.

Have one account for e-mails to go to so that librarians aren't all checking for patron messages and a patron isn't getting barraged by "out-of-office" answers. With a single e-mail address and a single password, all questions can be covered. Whoever reads it can also forward it to the department or person who can respond to it best. Centralization can be a big time-saver, and it encourages people to keep track of what's been answered and what hasn't. Putting answered or forwarded messages in folders can keep the account from becoming cluttered.

Commercial systems may do all of that for you, but you can do it all yourself, too. It takes a little longer and more attention to detail, but librarians are good at that. If you are at a small library, that may be all you need, and it will be cost effective.

Your website should have any limitations that are on your e-mail reference service, such as hours and amounts and reply times to expect. It should also address privacy concerns, such as retention times or use of personal information. You may or may not want to require a name as well as an e-mail address, depending on your policies. You should also spell out any limitations on your service area since e-mails are easy to send en masse. You can't identify the location that your patron is e-mailing from, but the polite ones will respect your limits. The ones who don't will e-mail anyway, but you can refer them to local libraries for answers.

You want to either have a form with required or optional information spaces or have the information you need on the Web page that has the reference e-mail address. Getting information in advance will save many e-mail exchanges and make the transaction move much faster. Some patrons may not want to give you all the information, so it's good to mark the information that's essential, like contact and subject information and what is optional but helpful.

The information you want to get in advance includes the following:

- Name
- Preferred e-mail (people may want to get the answer at their home account)
- Affiliation (are they in your service area or group?)
- Subject of research: the basic question
- Purpose
- Deadline
- Type and amount of material
- Who the patron is (a professor, a fifth grader?)
- Where did the patron hear about the subject?
- What time period should be covered?
- What format should the answer be in?

Answers for common questions can go into your wiki or frequently-asked-questions site since you've already answered them in print. That's one advantage of e-mail to phone from the librarian's point of view. You don't have to key the answer twice, and you can share them easily. You can also save them in a database where you or patrons can search them, but do remember to update them if the answer is likely to change and date the answer. An advantage of a frequently-asked-question site is that you can list the URL where you found the answer and periodically use a link checking site to make sure that the URL is still live. It won't tell you if the information has changed, but it can take one more task off your list.

If you can't mail or fax photocopies and the patron will have to pick them up or the material is too fragile or too large to photocopy, let patrons know that early in the process. They may well decline them. Can you scan or photograph them and send them by attachment? That may depend on your resources and copyright policies, but that's an option to think about. Digitization driven by patron requests is a good way to construct a website, especially if you have paraprofessional to do that for you. People expect to find all their information online, so if you can repurpose your efforts with minimal expense, take the opportunity to do so.

Use a descriptive subject line in your response. An e-mail with the subject "re:" will likely not be opened or will be stopped by a spam filter. You can also use a less friendly but efficient subject line, like "Reply from Big Public Library," if you have an automated system to give an acknowledgment of receipt or have large volumes of e-mails to answer.

Use a greeting like you would in a letter. Use the patron's name if you have it since home accounts may be used by the whole family. It also personalizes your reply, and you want to start building a relationship since it's very likely that you will exchange several e-mails before getting all the information you need and getting the patron the information he needs.

You should avoid abbreviations, acronyms, and jargon, or you'll have to send more e-mails to explain them. Avoid any emoticons other than, maybe, a smiley in your signature block since you don't know the age of your patron (Krohn 2004). Always give full source information, without abbreviations, from the on-line public access catalog record. If you include a URL, put it on a separate line in case the patron needs to copy and paste it.

Keep your instructions and reply easy and simple. Don't try to be witty or funny; keep your response closer to business style than personal. Your policies will determine whether you sign the e-mail or use a signature block from the common account, but it should welcome the patron back if he needs clarification or more information, just like you would for an in-person interview.

Add an invitation to e-mail back again to your e-mail signature block. That can save some keystrokes and prevent you from forgetting to do so. Add you phone number too since that may be a time-saver once the patron realizes that you need more information than he provided.

There is a temptation to cut and paste an answer from the source. That may be all right for ready-reference questions if you include the citation. For subscription databases, that may be a violation of your contract. In that case, you'll need to check whether the patron is entitled to use the database under your contract, give him instructions to log on, and give detailed instructions on how to find the cited item.

The same temptation arises with Web pages. Remember that all Web pages are copyrighted whether they say so or not. It's better (and easier) to send the URL and let patrons check the source themselves.

By this time, you should know the basics of netiquette. Don't use all caps, use spell-check, and don't say anything you wouldn't want repeated all over the Web. Patrons may forward the e-mail to friends or family who can use the information, and you want to give a professional impression.

FAX

Fax used to be the height of technology, but its popularity is waning. It is still a useful tool in the reference interview in special cases. Fax is usually used for reference only when an image is important for the interview. If picture is worth a thousand words, it is worth 10,000 keystrokes. If it's not important to the interview, phone or e-mail will be faster and easier.

People often don't leave the fax machine at home on all the time, so ask when you should send it or if you should call ahead. Businesses usually leave it on overnight, so you can send a fax after business hours. Many computers have fax functions, but the patron may not know that or how they work. You can always refer patron to their software manuals or help files, but it may be just as fast and simple to send a file via FTP or an e-mail attachment.

In other facets of the interview, fax is no different than e-mail and can be treated like it. The major difference is to use a cover sheet, which will literally cover the information while it is printing for confidentiality and contain any other information you need to include. Have a cover sheet that you can photocopy or a template on your computer that contains all the incidental information you want your patron to have. It saves many keystrokes, and a letterhead spreads your library's "brand."

REFERENCES

Krohn, F. B. "A Generational Approach to Using Emoticons as Nonverbal Communication." *Journal of Technical Writing and Communication* 34, no. 4 (2004): 321–28.
Ohio Reference Excellence. "Telephone and Email Reference." 2008 http://www.olc.org/ore/3phone.htm (accessed July 13, 2010). Tips from their online training.

FURTHER READINGS

Abels, Eileen. "The E-mail Reference Interview." *RQ* 35, no. 3 (Spring 1996): 345–58.
Bowman, V. "The Virtual Librarian and the Electronic Reference Interview." *Internet Reference Services Quarterly* 7, no. 3 (2002): 3–14.
Bristow, Ann. "Academic Reference Service over E-Mail: An Update." *College and Research Libraries News* 53 (November 1992): 631–32.
Bristow, Ann, and Mary Buecheley. "Academic Reference Service over E-Mail: An Update." *C&RL News* 57, no. 7 (July/August 1995): 459–62.
Bushallow-Wilber, Lara, Gemma De Vinney, and Fritz Whitcomb. "Electronic Mail Reference Service: A Study." *RQ* 35 (Spring 1996): 359–71.
Collins, Susan L. "Location Is Everything: The Use and Marketing of Reference E-Mail." *Public Services Quarterly* 2, no. 1 (2006): 5–20.
Doherty, J. J. "Reference interview or reference dialogue?" *Internet Reference Services Quarterly* 11, no. 3 (2006): 95–107.
Fishman, Diane. "Managing the Virtual Reference Desk: How to Plan an Effective Reference E-Mail System." *Medical Reference Services Quarterly* 17, no. 1 (Spring 1998): 1–11. The experiences of the University of Maryland at Baltimore Health Sciences Library with e-mail reference in a medical setting.
Garnsey, Beth A., and Ronald R. Powell. "Electronic Mail Reference Service in the Public Library." *Reference & User Services Quarterly* 39 (2000): 245–54.

Lee, I. J. "Do Virtual Reference Librarians Dream of Digital Reference Questions? A Qualitative and Quantitative Analysis of Email and Chat Reference." *Australian Academic & Research Libraries* 35, no. 2 (2004): 95–110.

Leykam, Andrew, and Catherine Perkins. "Is This the Right Tool for Our Library? A Look at E-Mail Virtual Reference Use Patterns." *The Reference Librarian* 48, no. 1 (2008): 1–17.

Mabry, C. H. "The Reference Interview as Partnership: An Examination of Librarian, Library User, and Social Interaction." *The Reference Librarian* 83/84 (2003): 41–56.

Ross, Catherine Sheldrick, Kirsti Nelson, and Patricia Dewdney. *Conducting the Reference Interview: A How-to-Do-It Manual for Librarians.* New York: Neal-Schuman, 2002.

Stacy-Bates, Kristine. "Ready-Reference Resources and E-Mail Reference on Academic ARL Web Sites." *Reference & User Services Quarterly* 40, no. 1 (Fall 2000): 61–73.

Taher, M. "The Reference Interview through Asynchronous E-Mail and Synchronous Interactive Reference: Does It Save the Time of the Interviewee?" *Internet Reference Services Quarterly* 7, no. 3 (2002): 23–34.

Tomaiuolo, Nicholas, and Joan Packer. "Aska Do's, Don'ts, and How-To's: Lessons Learned in a Library." *Searcher* 8, no. 3 (March 2000): 32–35. The problems of e-mail reference, including anonymous users and minimal information. Tips include clearly stating the service limits and providing information equal to that given at the physical reference desk.

7 YOUR ABILITIES WITH DISABILITIES

Don't think you don't have patrons with disabilities. You do, no matter where you work and who you work with. The indications may not be as obvious as a white cane or a wheelchair. The disability may not be permanent, just a forgotten pair of reading glasses or a broken leg. Think about your life—your broken arm, your grandmother's walker, your uncle's arthritis, or your father's cataracts. Advocates often say to think of yourself as "temporarily able"—it may change at any time.

So lesson 1 is don't assume that everyone is equally able. They might not have taught you this in library school, but you should have learned it from life, and it will serve you well in your life.

Lesson 2 is that you need to give equal service to all your patrons. That's part of the American Library Association code and part of your mission.

Think of reference service to people with disabilities as just being polite. Your attitude will be communicated by your body language and actions. If you suspect that someone is having problems with your library physically, ask how you can help or unobtrusively do so. "Unobtrusively" is the key word here. Make it as normal as opening a door for someone whose hands are full. You don't want to rush in and help someone who doesn't need help. Most people with disabilities manage quite well on their own and are offended when you rush in and help without asking if they need it. Don't be surprised if they refuse your help.

We know that many people are intimidated by libraries, especially academic ones. Imagine how much more intimidating they are when you can't physically access the information they hold. I've often heard librarians say, "We don't have any disabled patrons." What they are really saying is, "Our library and librarians are so inaccessible and unwelcoming that people with disabilities don't even come here." You may have made your library physically accessible under the law, but are your librarians as open?

There are more than 75 million Americans with disabilities, a number that will grow as the baby boomers age. Many disabilities are age related, such as cataracts and hearing loss, and as such will grow as that age-group grows but remains active.

They are not the only people with disabilities, though. Some children are born with them, some people acquire them through illness or accident, and some have undiagnosed disabilities. The last is particularly true of learning disabilities, like dyslexia, that affect library use. You will have patrons who have the same needs and desires to use the library as everyone else but cannot use print or who read at a low level. Not all disabilities have any outward sign.

There are advocacy and disability organizations in every state and many communities that you can invite to help review your services and facilities. They can make suggestions and offer training for your staff. You can do empathy training in-house at minimal cost. If you have staff who are nearsighted, take away their glasses for a few hours. Wear earmuffs for a while and see how people treat you. Use crutches or bandage your knees to see how difficult it is to get around in your library. Spend your day wearing mittens. Actually experiencing the difficulties, especially when the disabilities are visible, can give you a much better understanding of your patrons' experience in the library.

If your library has assistive aids, make sure that you know where they are and that they have good signage and instructions. Someone (if not everyone) on your staff should know enough about them to teach patrons how to use them and to use them to conduct a reference interview. Someone should have the responsibility of updating the software and maintaining the hardware. Some aids are as simple as a good magnifier.

Don't worry about watching the figures of speech you use. "Let's walk over there," "So to speak," and "You see" are all expressions used by people with disabilities as well. You will be more offensive if you blush and stammer when you say it. Since you accompany patrons to the stacks to find items and adapt your reference interview to each patron, you should have no problems working with all your patrons. If you are the only librarian on duty and can't go to the stacks or if you have a disability yourself that precludes it, one of your staff can help out.

As more information is available online, some information becomes more accessible, but some becomes less so. You can't control other people's bad design, but you can control your own. Check your catalog and the databases you subscribe to for accessibility (W3C). Your responsibility is to get information to patrons. You can't do that with bad website design any more than you can with badly printed books. You're the one who works with the patrons, so you see what the problems are. You can always let the person who really has the power to make changes know, but such people are seldom the ones working with the patrons. You are.

Accessibility is mandated by law for any organization recieving federal funds, and it's just good manners. Your state may have funds available for accessibility aids and software, so ask about it. You can also get help with training for your staff.

There is a large amount of literature and a good amount of online freeware for making your services available to everyone (Library Success 2010). There are books and workshops aimed at just libraries.

If you can't get the information to your patrons—if you can't ask them what they need—it's affecting your job, too. Remember that you too are only temporarily able bodied, and every step you take to make your library more accessible makes it more accessible to everyone.

COMPANION ANIMALS

Not everyone who is visually impaired has a guide dog, and not all companion animals belong to visually impaired people. They are often used by people with mobility issues, too, and not all companion animals are dogs. Monkeys are smart and agile, making them perfect assistants. Cats are loyal friends to people with anxiety disorders.

Companion animals are not required to wear any identification, so if your library doesn't allow pets and someone says that the animal is a service animal, take him at his word. If a patron approaches you and says that he's afraid of dogs or has allergies, help him find another place to work. In the case of fear of dogs, walking past the dog with the patron can allay the fear.

Don't pet or feed a companion animal. They are working and trained to take that very seriously. They will ignore you; don't take it personally. Don't tell them to sit or any other action; not only will they ignore you, but it's rude to their owners. If you really cannot help yourself, you can ask the owner if it's okay to pet the dog or if it needs something that you can get, but expect the answer to be "no." Companion animals are very good at letting their owners know what they need and vice versa.

PRINT AND VISUAL DISABILITIES

Not all people with visual impairment use a white cane or read Braille; in fact, most don't. Nor are all people with visual impairments blind; many have partial sight, but it may be only one part of their visual field. They may have poor vision overall but good vision at close range.

Always introduce yourself, at least by title or function, when the patron approaches the desk and ask how you can help—don't make any assumptions based on an apparent disability. When you move away or are working at your computer, tell the person so that he knows what you are doing. Imagine if you were in a store and the clerk disappeared—that's the effect of the nonverbal librarian.

Resist the temptation to talk louder to a visually impaired person. It's annoying and makes you look silly, something most of us try to avoid. If you need to get a patron's attention and don't know his name, touch his arm gently. Get up and go around the desk if you need to. Since visually impaired patrons rely on your voice to convey information, be aware of the noise level and move to a quieter area if needed.

When you lead a patron to an area, let him take your arm—don't take his. You want to lead, not steer, the patron. If the patron seems hesitant, just ask if he would like to take your arm. Generally, your voice will guide him to where your arm is, but remember that when you don't talk, you disappear. You can use the usual social small talk or a comment on the weather or a book the patron is asking about.

Ask if someone has a preferred format, but don't assume that he's looking for Braille or talking books. Don't overlook print, as there are many electronic options, like scanners with optical character recognition that can be used with screen readers. Large print may be preferred by people with low vision. Give the patron the option of picking from all the formats you hold.

You should keep track of any conflicts with your holdings and common accessibility software that you hear of. Some e-book formats work only with certain devices or systems. Don't assume that Google Books will be helpful since they may not work with screen readers; however, e-book readers are becoming inexpensive enough that you may want to have several for patrons with disabilities. If you have handouts, make them available online for people who use screen readers and in large print.

Many digital collections, especially ones of historical documents, are images of text and are not accessible by screen readers. You can help all patrons by sending a note to the institution explaining the situation. It doesn't hurt to point out that there are laws, including the Americans with Disabilities Act and the Canadian Charter of Rights and Freedoms, requiring public institutions to make websites accessible, and your library's site should be accessible as well.

If you hold popular videos, order them with both captioning and verbal descriptions. These are also useful for people who are learning the language, so it's generally a good practice to order them with all the capabilities you can. They will be used long after they are the current favorite if they can be used in different ways later.

Dyslexia is a cognitive and not a visual impairment, but it functions like one. It is often used to cover a range of cognitive problems, so don't assume that means only "scrambled reading"; it may be "scrambled hearing" or "scrambled speech" or any language-processing disorder. Never think that these patrons are less intelligent for having this disorder; they are often intelligent and have been making their own adaptations for years.

As a processing disorder, dyslexia can affect handwriting and spelling. This can be an issue for e-mail or chat reference since spell-checkers make notoriously bad guesses. If a question doesn't seem to make sense, like "How do you make trial mix?," or you need to clarify it, try to use words that are not easily confused.

Dyslexic patrons may not know that they are qualified to use the Talking Books program, so you may want to drop that option into your suggestions. The application for services is available through the Library of Congress's National Library Service for the Blind and Physically Handicapped. In Canada, services are available through the Canadian National Institute for the Blind. Canada, the United States, and Great Britain have postal subsidies for postage for materials for the print disabled, so there are no costs associated with them, although there may be time lags.

Books on tape and CD—or now on USB drives—are useful for all your patrons who may listen to them while driving or at work. Remember that "books" means information, not just a paper volume, so think about the media that's useful for your patron and not just the content.

HEARING IMPAIRMENT

Like visual impairment, hearing impairment represents a spectrum of functional loss. Hearing loss can be in only one part of the range, so a patron may be able to understand speech in a particular register but not another. Perhaps a man's low voice is easier to understand than a woman's high one or vice versa. If another librarian is requested, it may simply be that your voice is more difficult to understand. Don't take it personally.

If a patron has a hearing aid or a cochlear implant, don't assume that means he can understand you. He can hear you, but that's another matter. Hearing aids may not help with all parts of a hearing problem, just certain parts. Cochlear implants are not hearing aids; rather, they translate sound into other things that have to interpreted by the patron. They give him clues to the sounds, but those clues are not what you hear.

Like visual impairment, all people are different. Some people lip-read, some don't. Some speak, some don't. Don't assume that everyone does everything, as there are many variables, such as the age at which one's hearing becomes impaired. Someone who loses hearing late in life may speak but not lip-read, and the opposite may be true for persons who lose hearing at a young age.

One thing applies in all situations: don't stand with your back to a strong light source, like a window or bright light. That puts the light in the patron's eyes, making it difficult to see your face. If you see the patron squint, move to one side or to another area with better lighting.

Despite the popular perception, few people who have hearing loss lip-read. Lipreading is a very difficult skill that takes years to master and doesn't replace hearing since you have to face the patron at all times. It does help, however; so don't turn away from people with hearing loss. For persons who don't lip-read, your face still provides clues to words that are difficult to distinguish and lets them know when you have finished speaking. While you shouldn't turn your back on any patron without an explanation, be concious of explaining why before you turn away.

Don't talk louder unless someone asks you to; for people with hearing aids, it can cause feedback and actually be painful. Don't overarticulate, as that can make both hearing and lipreading more difficult.

Don't use idioms, jargon, or slang. The patron may know them, but it will slow things down if you have to explain, just as it can in other situations.

Speak in short sentences, not complex ones. They are easier to follow and easier for an interpreter to translate.

Some seniors are still coming to grips with hearing loss and don't admit to it. They may accuse you of mumbling or whispering. Don't argue the point; you may want to own it. Saying, "I'm sorry, I have a cold" or "I'm sorry, I have laryngitis, let me write it out for you," not only gives them a graceful and nonconfrontational out but also makes you partners rather than adversaries.

SIGNING

If a patron comes with an interpreter, look at the patron and not the interpreter. It's not being rude to them; it's an expected part of the job. Your patron is the person who will use the information. The interpreter is usually a few words behind the patron, so don't let that throw you off.

Don't hesitate to write your question or to ask the patron to write questions if necessary. Paper and pencil are assistive aids, too. You can do the whole reference interview on paper faster than by playing charades—and with less embarrassment to either party. Writing also allows some confidentiality that isn't available when speaking—a handy tip for any reference interview. Write important words as you speak so that the patron can both follow you and correct you if necessary. Keep the paper in plain view all the time so that the patron can follow you.

While many hearing-impaired patrons don't sign, many do know finger spelling. Finger spelling is easy to learn, and even if you use it only to spell difficult words, it can make communication much easier. It's worth spending an hour or two learning it.

Films and videos should include captioned materials, which are also popular with people learning languages. If video materials aren't marked on the packaging, you might want to have a sticker as well as making sure it's apparent from the cataloging.

You may want to ask if someone in your library knows sign language. You may be surprised. Many people have family members, friends, or neighbors from whom they learned sign language. Some communities have translator services, or you can call a local college and see if it has a translation service. This is true of foreign languages, too.

Your patron may also not be a native English speaker. That will complicate the situation but is not impossible to deal with. You use writing to communicate with non-English speakers, and you can do it with this patron as well. He may not be able to follow your facial expressions if he's reading, too, so leave a little time for him to read. Generally, the patron will look up when he's done; then you can pick up the transaction again.

Patrons who attended schools for the hearing impaired often have less experience and training in using libraries than the general population, so be prepared for more instruction than usual in upper grades and in college (Locke 1997). You may want to engage an interpreter and do group instruction in the fall at the start of a new school year. You can do it at any time of the year in a public library, and it will be appreciated. Informal instruction should be offered when you see the need for it, just like any other patron.

MOBILITY IMPAIRMENT

Like other disabilities, there is a range of mobility impairment but much wider than a single sense. To complicate things, such impairments may come and go with time or other circumstances. Like all of us, people have good days and bad ones, except it may be good weeks or bad months. Some conditions leave the patron generally weak so that he can do anything but not for long.

Never move the patron's wheelchair without asking. That's the equivalent of shoving him out of the way. If a patron moves to a chair to work, don't move his wheelchair or crutches. He left them where he did because he wants to access them again without help, and you have just made him dependent on you. Remember that you're trying to be polite and helpful to him, not yourself.

There are two things you should never do when your patron uses a wheelchair. Never lean on the chair while you're talking; that's part of his personal space and is like someone sitting on your lap. Never pat someone who uses a wheelchair on the head or shoulder. That's patronizing. You may not realize you're doing it, as you may be used to working with children at that height, but it's very offensive. Imagine a basketball player patting you on the head like a pet because you're short, and you'll get the feeling.

When it's apparent that someone has difficulty walking or reaching, offer to get materials or have someone go with him to browse. If you do that routinely, you can explain that, but it still may be percieved as patronizing or unneeded. Again, offer help but don't assume that they will accept it or that they need it.

If a patron uses a wheelchair, move to his level. A service desk, if you have one, should have two levels, but if it doesn't, pull up a chair or invite the patron to a nearby table. Like all your patrons, you want to be able to make eye contact at a comfortable level for both of you. There's a reason for phrases like "looking up" to someone or "looking down" on someone; those are the feelings you evoke when you are literally at different levels. You want to be partners in the search, not imply levels of authority.

Again, ask if the patron has a preferred format. If a patron has arthritis, he may prefer an audio book or an abridged edition that is more lightweight. On the other hand, the patron may have a great reading stand at home and prefer full editions. Offer the patron the options that you have and let him make the decisions.

If a patron seems to have difficulty standing while you talk, pull up a chair or move someplace more comfortable. You can sit, too; you want to stay at the patron's eye level. A chair nearby will come in handy when modeling seraching, too.

When a patron uses crutches or a walker, you may want to offer to hold his books at the desk until he's ready to check out. It's very difficult to juggle several books while browsing when your hands are already busy. Some libraries use the handheld baskets that are used at grocery stores; these make it easier for anyone—mothers with children, heavy readers, or the disabled—to carry their books to the checkout.

SPEECH IMPAIRMENT

Stuttering and stammering are the most familiar impediments, but people may also have facial paralysis or dental problems that make their speech hard to understand. Never confuse a speech impairment with an intellectual or mental one. They may coexist, but they are definitely not related. If you've ever received pitying looks from strangers when you left the dentist mumbling, you know how people can misunderstand more than your speech.

People with hearing disabilities may also have speech issues since they may not be able to hear what they are saying. If you have difficulty understanding a word, just say so and offer a pencil and paper for the patron to write it. In both speech and lipreading, certain letters are difficult to distinguish: "p" from "b," "g" from "d," and so on. Ask if the patron knows finger spelling, which can help him get past words that trigger stuttering. Or you can just listen more closely. It's your problem, not his.

Never try to finish a sentence for a person, as that's both rude and frustrating. Maintain eye contact and let him finish. When you try to finish a sentence, you are putting words in the patron's mouth without knowing what he was saying.

If you need to have a person write down his question or repeat it, you may want to take ownership of the communication problem. "I'm sorry, could you repeat that? I seem to be having problems today with the background noise." Pick the applicable problem of your choice—a crying child, a head cold, or echoes if the room is empty. It will put the person at ease and may make communication easier.

INTELLECTUAL DISABILITIES

More than 7 million Americans (or 3% of the U.S. population) have an intellectual disability. To put that in terms that apply to your library, if you have a patron base of only 1,000 people, 30 will have an intellectual disability. You may have as many patrons with an IQ of 75 as with an IQ of 125, but they may not feel as welcome in your library. You may never know who they are since there may not be any visible sign. People with minor intellectual disabilities have spouses and children, families and friends, and jobs and driver's licenses. They are your neighbors and your patrons.

As mentioned before, people are people. Don't treat an adult with retardation like a child, but you may want to use the same skills you do with younger people. Avoid jargon and try to use the same words for the same things consistently. Try to determine what level materials the person is looking for and use the same question negotiation skills as elsewhere. Don't assume that the person is looking for the same subjects that a child is; they are adults and have the same interests as other adults. Offer easier reading levels but don't insist on it, as they may have excellent reading skills but be delayed in other areas (Walling 2001).

Offer to search for the patron and show them how to search and use online tools like renewals. Information literacy skills, which are rarely taught in school classes for these patrons, can be helpful. On the other hand, they may be as uninterested as other patrons may be.

Tape-and-text materials, high-interest/low-vocabulary materials, and audio books are formats that you can offer. Many formats bought for one type of patron, like high-interest/low-vocabulary materials intended for patrons learning English, may be welcome to patrons with intellectual disabilities. Larger print and clear fonts make reading easier for all groups.

Signing conventions and jargon may be confusing, so offer to accompany people to the stacks to locate materials. Your space should use universal symbols as part of your signage; this will help all your patrons find restrooms and phones.

It's not unusual for people to have multiple disabilities, so don't make assumptions about vision or mobility for this group that you wouldn't make for others.

MENTAL ILLNESS

Mental illness is another field where there are many misconceptions and stereotypes. Few people who are mentally ill are also violent. Depression is the most common mental illness, and few librarians will complain about patrons being too sedate and quiet. People who are mentally ill are often intelligent, so don't treat them as if they aren't. Sometimes it's simply eccentricity; wearing red and purple is even a sign of group membership for older women and is not really eccentric at all. Sometimes the older man who talks loudly and doesn't seem to understand what you're saying really has a hearing problem. Once again, be polite and don't make assumptions; it may not be an issue in the interview at all.

Be nonjudgmental and ask lots of questions to clarify what patrons are really looking for. Sometimes what they want may not exist, like Lincoln's baby pictures; simply tell them that you don't have it. You can offer the earliest known image and books they can check. Don't argue history; it's most likely that they're looking at the library because, like most of us, they trust what they see in print.

Sometimes patrons will know what they want, but it may take them a while to tell you. Their conversation may wander, but you can bring them back by asking again what exactly they're looking for or restating their request: "So we're looking for something on cat breeds. This one looks good . . . "

It's likely that you will identify some people who are poorly groomed as mentally ill, but that's not a safe assumption to make. Sometimes it's a fashion or political statement, and sometimes it's a matter of resources. Sometimes an odor is a result of a medical condition and not lack of cleanliness; you wouldn't (or shouldn't) assume that someone who uses a wheelchair is mentally ill, so why distinguish what offends you as the result of mental illness?

The best thing a library can do for people with disabilities is staff training, not just for reference librarians but for all staff who meet the public. Other people can read body language and expressions as well (or better) than librarians and can tell if you are uncomfortable around them. Much of that discomfort is the result of ignorance, stereotypes, and misconceptions. Not only advocacy groups in your area but also your staff can do training. Encourage them to share their experiences with friends and relatives with disabilities, and you all can lose your fear of "others."

REFERENCES

Library Success. "Website Design" (wiki). http://www.libsuccess.org/index.php?title=Website _Design (accessed October 12, 2010).

Locke, B. M. "Libraries and the Deaf: They Can Read Books Can't They?" *Sound News* 15, no. 1 (1997): 5–6.

Walling, Linda Lucas, comp. *Library Services to the Sandwich Generation and Serial Caregivers.* Chicago: American Library Association, 2001.

FURTHER READING

Alexander, Linda Baldwin. "ADA resources for the library and information professions." *Journal of Education for Library and Information Science* 46 (Summer 2005): 248–57.

Alter, Rachel, Linda Walling, Susan Beck, Kathleen Garland, Ardis Hanson, and Walter Metz. *Guidelines for Library Services for People with Mental Illnesses.* Chicago: American Library Association, 2007.

Association of Specialized and Cooperative Library Agencies. *Guidelines for Library and Information Services for the American Deaf Community.* Chicago: American Library Association, 1996.

Association of Specialized and Cooperative Library Agencies. "Library Services for People with Disabilities Policy." http://www.ala.org/ala/mgrps/divs/ascla/asclaissues/ libraryservices.cfm (accessed October 20, 2010).

Association of Specialized and Cooperative Library Agencies. *Revised Standards and Guidelines of Service for the Library of Congress Network of Libraries for the Blind and Physically Handicapped.* Chicago: American Library Association, 2005.

Association of Specialized and Cooperative Library Agencies. *Standards Committee Subcommittee to Develop Guidelines for Library Services at Institutions for People with Mental Retardation.* Chicago: American Library Association, 1999.

Bernstein, Neil. *Flash-Memory Distribution of Digital Talking Books.* Washington, DC: National Library Service for the Blind and Physically Handicapped, Library of Congress, 2005. Also available at http://www.loc.gov/nls/technical/flashdistribution.html.

Creaser, Claire, J. Eric Davies, and Stella Wisdom. "Accessible, Open and Inclusive: How Visually Impaired People View Library and Information Services and Agencies." *Journal of Librarianship and Information Studies* 34, no. 4 (2002): 207–14.

DO-IT. "Working Together: Computers and People with Learning Disabilities" (video, 2002). http://www.washington.edu/doit/Video/wt_learn.html.

EASI. "Library Resources." http://people.rit.edu/easi/lib.htm (accessed September 29, 2010). Library and information technology resources for accessibility.

Epp, Mary Ann. "Closing the 95% Gap: Library Resource Sharing for People with Print Disabilities." *Library Trends* 54, no. 3 (Winter 2006): 411–29.

Hannah, K. "Developing Accessible Library Services." *Library and Information Update* 2, no. 11 (2003): 50–52.

Hernon, Peter, and Philip Calvert, eds. *Improving the Quality of Library Services for Students with Disabilities*. Westport, CT: Greenwood Press, 2006.

Jennerich, Elaine Z., and Edward J. Jennerich. *The Reference Interview as a Creative Art*. 2nd ed. Westport, CT: Libraries Unlimited, 1997.

Kinder, Sean. "Web Page Accessibility for Users with Disabilities." *Kentucky Libraries* 65, no. 4 (Fall 2001): 21–22.

Kirkpatrick, Cheryl H. "Getting Two for the Price of One: Accessibility and Usability." *Computers in Libraries* 23, no. 1 (January 2003): 26–29.

Lewis, Valerie, and Julie Klauber. "[Image] [Image] [Image] [Link] [Link] [Link]: Inaccessible Web Design from the Perspective of a Blind Librarian." *Library Hi Tech* 20, no. 2 (2002): 137–40.

McKenna, Janet. "Huh? What? Interacting with Your Hard of Hearing Patrons." *Public Libraries* 42 (January–February 2003): 9–11.

"Meeting the Need" (video). Washington, DC: Library of Congress, National Library Service for the Blind and Physically Handicapped, Publications and Media Section, 1994.

National Library Service for the Blind and Physically Handicapped. http://www.loc.gov/nls.

Nielsen, Gyda Skat, and Birgitta Irvall. "Guidelines for Library Services to Persons with Dyslexia." IFLA Professional Reports, no. 70 (2001). http://www.ifla.org/VII/s9/nd1/iflapr-70e.pdf. Also available in Spanish as IFLA Professional Reports no. 76 and in French as IFLA Professional Reports no. 74.

NLS Reference Bibliographies. "Library and Information Services for Blind and Physically Handicapped Individuals" (2006). http://www.loc.gov/nls/reference/bibliographies/library.html (accessed October 21, 2010).

Norton, Melanie J. "Effective Bibliographic Instruction for Deaf and Hearing-Impaired College Students." *Library Trends* 41, no. 1 (Summer 1992): 118–50.

Peters, Tom, and Lori Bell. "Hello IM, Goodbye TTY." *Computers in Libraries* 26 (May 2006): 18–21.

Playforth, Sarah. "Inclusive Library Services for Deaf People: An Overview from the Social Model Perspective." *Health Information and Libraries Journal* 21, suppl. 2 (2004): 554–57.

Polanka, Sue, and Jack O'Gorman. "Guidelines for Creating Accessible Library Web Pages." *Internet Reference Services Quarterly* 5, no. 3 (2001): 51–57.

Rodriguez, Rosa, and Monica Reed. "Our Deaf Family Needs to Read, Too." *Public Libraries* 42 (January–February 2003): 38–41.

Rubin, Rhea Joyce. *Planning for Library Services to People with Disabilities*. Chicago: American Library Association, 2001.

Schmetzke, Axel. "Accessibility of Web-Based Information Resources for People with Disabilities." *Library Hi Tech* 20 (2002): 135–231. The entire issue is devoted to accessibility issues.

Schmetzke, Axel. "Web Accessibility at University Libraries And Library Schools." *Library Hi Tech* 19, no. 1 (2001): 35–49.

Walling, Linda Lucas, and Marilyn M. Irwin. *Information Services for People with Developmental Disabilities: The Library Manager's Handbook*. Westport, CT: Greenwood Press, 1995.

Web Accessibility Initiative W3C. http://www.w3.org/WAI. The W3C provides a validator for HTML at http://validator.w3.org and one for CSS at http://jigsaw.w3.org/css-validator.

8 VIRTUAL REFERENCE IN SECOND LIFE AND VIRTUAL WORLDS

SECOND LIFE

Is it time for you to MUVE into virtual reality? MUVEs are multiple-user virtual environments, and Second Life is among the best known.

If you're not familiar with Second Life, think of it as Facebook on steroids. You chat, but you can also read books, build a house, and fly. In Second Life, you can chat by text or Voice over Internet Protocol (VoIP), although not everyone has VoIP technology. Second Life runs on an application that users download to their computers (this may cause issues with your information technology department). You can create your avatar and change it when you want to. There are gestures available, so you can wave at patrons or sit down to talk. When you type a message, your avatar is animated to type, too, so there is less of the awkward pause when answering questions.

Libraries and librarians exist there, as do many people who may be our patrons. It's a great place to collaborate. It also has a steep learning curve and takes a lot of bandwidth. You will not find many of your users in Second Life, as they are likely in the physical library asking questions because they don't care about virtual worlds, don't have high-powered computers, or don't have a fast connection. On the other hand, you will find a lot of potential patrons who don't go to the library at all.

Many of the questions asked at the Second Life reference desk are about Second Life, the assumption being that it's a help feature within Second Life. Since Second Life is a visual environment, you'll have to make it visually obvious that you're a real library service and not a Second Life one.

How are you identifying yourself as a reference librarian? Standing behind a desk doesn't work any better in a virtual world. Just like the real world, a big sign or a T-shirt works better. There are libraries and reference desks in Info

Archipelago, the library "island," or virtual location, but, as we all know, the desk isn't always the best place to connect with patrons.

You'll need to identify whether a patron can use your resources—whether he is one of your patrons in reality—because of licensing restrictions. That needs to be the first question of your interview. A virtual world would be a great place to work together, but the intricacies of licensing and working on another server may well leave your patron stranded. Proxy servers, pop-up windows, and all the other facts of online life will limit your ability to help the patron. You may be limited to free sites, which may be sufficient for your patron but won't give him the best service you can offer.

Second Life and other MUVES are not available to all your patrons. There is a high cost in bandwidth and hardware to access it and a considerable learning curve, and it is not friendly to disabled patrons. It is used increasingly as a teaching platform, though, and librarians can expect to be embedded the same as in Blackboard and other content management systems. In the same way as the traditional reference desk was in the middle of the collection, the virtual one must be as well.

Although Second Life is free to users, it's not entirely free. If you want to build a virtual space, you will have to buy real estate or rent it from someone who has purchased it. That makes it a continuing cost to provide space for your library. That is important because although you can wander around and offer to answer questions, you need a place where your patrons can connect with your service and not just your avatar. You may have several librarians who work the service, and you'll need a central contact point.

It's good that avatars are less shy about asking questions, but they're less inhibited in being rude and offensive, too. Expect more offensive questions than you get at a desk and be prepared to deal with them. You can also get pelted with virtual snowballs. Troublemakers are called "griefers" in Second Life, and they are there and may change their avatar's features and form between visits. You can check an avatar's profile in Second Life for previous problems. Ask avatars privately to behave or leave before doing it publicly. If that doesn't work, use the software to remove them.

In Second Life, you *really* cannot make assumptions about the patron. Nothing about the avatar need be really related to the patron behind it—not gender, not age, not species. Nor can the patron assume that you are really a librarian, not just a librarian avatar. Even within a virtual library, the person in the library is not necessarily a librarian or related to the library.

People will bring assumptions with them to Second Life, however. Avatars with more realistic faces will be regarded as more human and experienced than the cartoonish one or an animal, which may be regarded as less important or less experienced.

The reference interview is much like it is in chat reference; the virtual world doesn't add much at this point except gestures. If you both have VoIP systems, you can carry on a real-time interview, but don't plan on that. Besides the technical issues, it destroys the avatar's image when the hulking Viking speaks with the voice of a 12-year-old girl. You can carry on the reference interview the way that you would in a chat or instant messaging environment. Just like those environments, don't be surprised if your patron suddenly disappears. He may have transported elsewhere, or he may have lost his connection to the server. There can be other server issues to deal with, like freezing up and not being able to reply to questions.

Second Life has its own economy, driven by services and the creation of Second Life products, so don't be surprised if avatars ask how much it costs to answer a question. While Second Life itself is free, the "stuff" that makes it fun has a cost in the local virtual currency. Second Life has its own economy, and information can be a commodity there as well.

The library tends to draw social users as much as library users, so there is much more contact between the librarians and the patrons than in the real world. That means that you will have many distractions, and, like real life, you may want to move to a quieter area for the reference interview.

Second Life can be an event venue where authors can hold readings and book discussion groups can meet. It also works as an exhibit space. Second Life slide shows can serve as signs for services, classes, and hours when a librarian isn't in Second Life. Second Life can be a meeting place for orientation and information literacy sessions for distance education students if they have the technology and use Second Life otherwise. However, students will be reluctant to use Second Life for just one session if they have to learn a new system to do so.

Second Life is a 24/7 service, but librarians aren't. With volunteers from around the world, that may be a possibility, but it's unlikely that any library can afford the staff for extended hours. However, Second Life can be a great place for virtual meetings and collaborations. Imagine creating tutorials and having a native speaker translate them or a virtual library where patrons can see presentations and videos that are created in Second Life or created elsewhere but available in Second Life. You can have lessons or programming that appeals to younger people. You can have RSS feeds to keep people up to date on events.

Second Life is a young technology (launched in 2003) but one that suits many teaching needs as well as being used for virtual campus visits and donor contacts. Second Life may not be the last word in virtual worlds, but it follows the trend in the gaming world for multiuser online venues. More virtual world offerings are in the future, but the one that will allow a cloud-based venue will eliminate some of the current limitations.

Think of Second Life as a platform for the services you already offer. Think of an instant messaging service that has compatible software, RSS feeds to the same platform, and quick changes from text to audio chat. Second Life is a taste of what may be coming along next.

Where Second Life excels is in doing things that are impossible physically. You can be an embedded librarian with a medical team during an epidemic. You can teach a student's avatar how to deal with emergencies and violent patrons. You can be an informationist on a lunar exploration expedition. You can lead a global seminar on reference services. The possibilities are endless, but the librarian's time is not. Keep in touch with people who are using Second Life and offer your services; however, it likely wouldn't be efficient to build the services and hope that people will use them.

By the time you read this, Second Life may be last year's new thing and something newer will have captured the collective librarian imagination. Second Life isn't a perfect place for us, but it is an interesting start to virtual worlds. It is a good place for teaching, but teachers have the control of the students' whereabouts. Librarians don't, and few students think of looking for information there. It's much cheaper in time and bandwidth to just log in to the library.

Virtual worlds have real advantages. You can think of Second Life as Asteroids compared with a modern gaming system. It's not the best, but if it's garnered this much interest, something better is sure to come along. Immersive and team-based games are still around, although you might not know that if you're not a gamer. Much of the virtual world is invisible if you're not looking for it, but it has a powerful draw, just like role-playing games. Only time will tell how we will use them and whether we use them.

FACEBOOK

Facebook, if you've been in a cave for the past few years or are over 40, is a social networking site that offers personal pages, RSS feeds from within the site, chat, ads, organizational pages, games, and, by the time you read this, something else: pages and posts from libraries and library groups and a simple question-and-answer service that is not a service for research questions but rather is useful for recommendations for leisure reading and ready-reference questions.

Facebook is a huge community, though, and if you post to the right place and the right people see it, you can get a large response. Like Flickr Commons, you can tap the knowledge of the masses but still have to evaluate it. Facebook, unlike Second Life, requires that you ask someone to be your "friend" or "like" them; thus, you don't get as many annoyances, but it is harder to build your base. Posting a message to your friends and asking them to spread the word is the best way to get noticed within Facebook, and letting people know outside Facebook can be done by ordinary means.

The largest "fan" base on Facebook is the Library of Congress, with 26,000 fans. That's not the best response rate. The Virtual Reference Desk has two fans. However, Facebook is a good place to put announcements, events, and news. You can put links to the other places you live on the Web on your home page. Your posts will appear on the news feed for your friends.

Facebook is a good place to advertise your services. You can post announcements, quizzes, or questions for responses—anything that keeps your "face" in the patron's mind. Invite your friends to instant message you, log onto a chat sessions, or come to your library in person.

An advantage of Facebook is that many people keep it open on their computer, so it is seen often during the day. If you post often enough, it can be like a poster on someone's desk. Facebook is not an immersive world like Second Life, though it does draw people into the space. It is mainly a social network where you can connect to friends.

Like the other virtual worlds and Web 2.0 technologies, you can spend a lot of time for small returns. On the other hand, you can grow the services if your patrons move to these newer technologies. If you already blog your services, you can copy your posts to Facebook with minimal effort.

EMBEDDED LIBRARIANS

You can be embedded anywhere that you can either access your resources or do a reference interview for later answers. That means you can be in a Blackboard course, in Facebook, in a department meeting, in a bookmobile, at a nursing home, at a branch far from the physical resources, or anywhere people go for information. You don't have to be there every moment of every day, but it's both a great outreach tool and a terrific way to make your services known and used.

The difference between an embedded librarian and a roaming one is that the embedded librarian is in the midst of your patrons, not just encountering them. The embedded librarian is part of a team that includes people who are not librarians. That can be an uncomfortable place for some of us, but it needn't be. You can be part of the teaching team in a distance class just like you are in a face-to-face one, except you are there when the students need you. You can be a part of a research team instead of an afterthought. You can be a player in the marketing department, not just a pawn. You can be more professional in an embedded role than any other, so don't let it intimidate you. This is what you got your graduate degree in—it's what you do.

Being a distance student, as more and more students are, means missing orientations and information literacy classes. It means a long trip to the library or even a short trip to someone else's library that doesn't have the resources that yours has. It means not knowing who the librarians are and finding the databases and how to use them by trial and error.

Embedded librarians are most commonly found in professional programs and in online course systems. In special libraries and professional schools, the librarian may be known as an informationist and may do reference on the fly during medical rounds. In a course management system like Blackboard, they may have regular hours in the system or be contacted within the system.

You can link to your services or resources within the system. The closer you are to the patron's point of need, the more likely they will be used and the more likely that you will be contacted. For some students, going outside the system is just as scary as going to the physical library. You can ease that by giving instructions and tutorials within the system.

Working within the system makes for some problems since subscription databases may not work within it and the librarian can't be online all the time. It does open up some opportunities, though. You can hold live tutorials for

THE REFERENCE INTERVIEW TODAY

students, you can answer questions later via another medium, and you can add links to resources referred to in the class. You can be part of a team within the class or part of a discussion group and offer expert sources to distant students. The discussion board or forum lets other users see your interview, or you can do it via the e-mail service within the system.

You can be physically embedded anywhere. You can be at a senior center one day, an Asian community center the next, and a day care center the next. You can be in touch with your patrons there between times by any method they choose and get information to them in the way they want it. It won't necessarily be instant gratification, but it will be convenient for the patrons. Many of these patrons can't or don't come to the physical library but will you use your services when you come to them.

You are an ambassador for the library. It will take different skills for different groups, but so does your physical library. The advantage is that you will have allies. The seniors will tell you what they've read in their reading groups, and you can plan what to read next. New arrivals will have people there who can help them express their needs in the reference interview without going through a translation service. You can help parents and teachers select books to read to children and help children with their homework.

When you have to get the information to the patron, you'll use the same techniques you do in any distance interview. Have a form that you or the patron can fill out with details so that you have that information when you need it. Have enough space that you can add details you learn in the interview. If you will check items out and deliver them to the patron, you'll need to have his library card number. You can e-mail the information to yourself or another staff member or use a paper form. If you need a signature, you'll need lots of paper forms:

- Date
- Patron's name
- Library card number
- Contact information
- Delivery method and/or delivery point

For known items, you'll need the following:

- Title
- Author
- Year

For reference requests, you'll need the following:

- Question
- Format for answer

- Amount of information needed
- Purpose of information
- Date needed
- Referral
- Sources checked
- Date of delivery
- Return date and return point
- Your name
- Notes

Reference librarians are used to being the go-to person for information; as embedded librarians you can be the proactive person for information needs. The patron's point of need is always with the patron but not always at the library. After all, the library isn't the books; it's the librarians who know how to get to the information.

Embedded librarians are most often found in colleges, but the principle applies everywhere. Find a group that needs information, talk to the leader, and find out what you can do. Then be there at the designated times and be reachable at others. In an academic library, that may make you a liaison. In a public library, you may be an outreach librarian. In a corporate library, you may be an informationist on a team. You can even be embedded in your own library as a training specialist. What makes you embedded is the fact that you are reliably available when you are needed. You are part of the group, not a one-time visitor.

You can be part of a book discussion groups that meets monthly, prepared with read-alikes and contextual information. You can be a member of the instructional team in an online class. The important part is that you are prepared to be a part of the exchange of information with the group and willing to continue that role.

FURTHER READING

Bell, Lori, Tom Peters, and Kitty Pope. "Get a (Second) Life! Prospecting for Gold in a 3-D World." *Computers in Libraries* 27, no. 1 (January 2007): 10–15.

Bell, Lori, K. Pope, and Tom Peters. "Digital Libraries on the MUVE: A Virtual Adventure." *Bulletin of the American Society of Information Science and Technology* 33, no. 4 (2007): 29.

Bell, Lori, and Rhonda B. Trueman, eds. *Virtual Worlds, Real Libraries. Librarians and Educators in Second Life and Other Multi-User Virtual Environments.* Medford, NJ: Information Today, 2008.

Blankenship, Emily F., and Yolanda Hollingsworth. "Balancing Both Lives: Issues Facing Librarians Working in Second Life and Real Life Worlds." *New Library World* 110, no. 9/10 (2009): 430–40.

Buckland, Amy, and Krista Godfrey. "Save the Time of the Avatar: Canadian Academic Libraries Using Chat Reference in Multi-User Virtual Environments." *The Reference Librarian* 51, no. 1 (2010): 12–30.

Condic, K. S. "Using Second Life as a Training Tool in an Academic Library." *The Reference Librarian* 50, no. 4 (October 2009): 333–45.

Eisenberg, M. "The Parallel Information Universe." *Library Journal* 133, no. 8 (2008): 22–25.

Erdman, J. "Reference in a 3-D Virtual World: Preliminary Observations on Library Outreach in 'Second Life.'" *The Reference Librarian* 47, no. 2 (July 2007): 29–39.

Foster, A. L. "The Avatars of Research." *Chronicle of Higher Education* 52, no. 6 (2005): A35–A36.

Ganster, Ligaya, and Bridget Schumacher. "Expanding beyond our Library Walls: Building an Active Online Community through Facebook." *Journal of Web Librarianship* 3, no. 2 (2009): 111–28.

Gerardin, J., M. Yamamoto, and K. Gordon. "Fresh Perspectives on Reference Work in Second Life." *Reference and User Services Quarterly* 47, no. 4 (2008): 324–30.

Godfrey, Krista. "A New World for Virtual Reference." *Library Hi Tech* 26, no. 4 (2008): 525–39. Second Life is the focus for these services. Advantages of virtual world reference are highlighted and drawbacks discussed.

Grassian, Esther, Rhonda B. Trueman, and Patrice Clemson. "Stumbling, Bumbling, Teleporting and Flying . . . Librarian Avatars in Second Life: Selected Bibliography." *Reference Services Review* 35, no. 1 (2007): 90–97.

Janes, Joe. "An Informal History (and Possible Future) of Digital Reference." *Bulletin of the American Society for Information Science and Technology* 34, no. 2 (December 2007/January 2008): 8–10.

Joint, Nicholas. "Virtual Reference, Second Life and Traditional Library Enquiry Services." *Library Review* 57, no. 6 (2008): 416–23.

Luo, Lili. "Reference Service in Second Life: An Overview." *Reference Services Review* 36, no. 3 (2008): 289–300.

Mathews, Brian. "Moving beyond the Reference Desk: Being Where Users Need Us." *The Reference Librarian* 48, no. 2 (2008): 9–13.

Peters, Tom. "Librarianship in Virtual Worlds." *Library Technology Reports* 44, no. 7 (2008): 1–32.

Stimpson, Jane D. "Public Libraries in Second Life." *Library Technology Reports* 45 (2009): 13–20.

Swanson, Kari. "Second Life: A Science Library Presence in Virtual Library." *Science & Technology Libraries* 27 (2007): 79–86.

Taher, Mohamed. "Real-Time (Synchronous Interactive) Reference Interview: A Select Bibliography." *Internet Reference Services Quarterly* 7, no. 3 (2002): 35–41.

Van Der Ven, Christian. "Second Life: A Tool for Reference and International Understanding." *The Reference Librarian* 49, no. 2 (September 2008): 149–61.

Westbrook, Lynn. "Virtual Reference Training: The Second Generation." *College & Research Libraries* 67, no. 3 (May 2006): 249–59.

Xia, David. "Marketing Library Services through Facebook Groups." *Library Management* 30, no. 6/7 (2009): 469–78.

9 FROM THEORY TO PRACTICE—NEW LIBRARIANS AND PARAPROFESSIONALS

One of the classic truths of an economic downturn is that more people will go back to school and more people will use public libraries while budgets are at their lowest. That puts a lot of pressure on librarians, who are expected to do more with less when they were already expected to do much with little. Paraprofessionals, staff, students, volunteers, and retirees may all be called on to help.

Paraprofessionals, trained people who work alongside the professionals, can handle many duties at the reference desk and beyond. They can help with programming in a public library, help patrons with software and hardware problems, extend your open hours, and add new subject knowledge to your team.

Tasks for nonlibrarians can include anything that takes some pressure off the librarians. Maybe the retired secretary will love to take and type meeting minutes, students will have great ideas for displays and take charge of them, graduate students will turn out great newsletters, and anyone can make copies for class sessions. Put a retired accountant to work maintaining your reference statistics, and you'll see them sliced, diced, and repurposed in ways that you can use.

While students often come in without any library skills, they have a vested interest in learning them. Their classes will require them, and they will need information skills beyond searching Google in future jobs. Learning the reference interview means that they have learned what they need for searching. Students are also more familiar with the technologies students use, from Blackboard to Second Life. They use them, too. They can give you insights into how students use them and how the reference interview can be constructed to work in them.

If your library is close to school that teaches library science or school librarianship, a quick call to the department may result in an internship or a practicum for a student. Even unpaid practicums are eagerly sought since they can give the student some real-life experience. It's worth taking a chance, even if it won't happen until the next term. You can offer practicums to other groups, too. History majors in archives, nursing students in medical libraries, and political

THE REFERENCE INTERVIEW TODAY

science students in law libraries will not only stretch your budget out but also give students experience that will help in their studies. All of them will need training and practice for reference work.

A large part of that is in the reference interview. Skipping the interview won't save time; rather, it wastes it, as you can spend your time answering the wrong question. Teaching it is the most important thing you can do for your library. For reference work, it's essential.

TEACHING THE REFERENCE INTERVIEW

Some people are born teachers. Most of us are born librarians and need a little help with our teaching skills. We know about patrons coming to us at their "point of need." In education, people talk about Piaget's "teachable moment" (Havighurst 1952). That moment happens when someone has the skills to learn something new. Without those skills and knowledge to build on, he won't learn the new skill. You have to stand before you can walk, walk before you can run. The principle applies to all learning.

People have different learning styles, too. While we think that all librarians and paraprofessionals must be very visual and print oriented since they work with print, that's not necessarily the best way for a particular person to learn. It's true of patrons, too. Some people learn best visually by reading. Some learn best by hearing something explained. Some people learn by doing. Others learn best by talking about a subject in a discussion. While most people have a preferred or dominant style, teaching reference is best taught by teaching things in several styles.

While slide presentations (real or virtual) are a popular way to train, they are in fact a bad one. Slides are a distraction from what you're saying. Just like the reference interview, people want to get clues from body language and expressions. That's not possible in a dark room or when they're distracted by slides. If you use slide shows, use them to illustrate what you're talking about, not to deliver what you're saying.

Videos are better since there are real people in them. There are a number of sources for videos, including the Library of Congress. YouTube has short videos on many types of interactions, including training for other fields. Many of the principles are the same in retail and medicine, so don't reinvent the wheel if you can avoid it.

The basics of teaching are giving the person the knowledge, demonstrating how it is used, and letting the students practice. In our case, we can give the student the knowledge in several ways, and you may want to do just that—offer it in several forms. Tell the student what he's going to learn and why, then give him the information. You can do that verbally, it can be in writing, it can be online, or it can be all three. Then discuss it and let him ask questions. Then he's ready to understand what he's seeing when you demonstrate it or when he observes someone else. Give him a chance to ask questions again to you or the person he's observing. At that point, he's ready to practice the skill he's learned with feedback from you.

That's the general procedure. Some skills may require more practice than reading, and some students need more feedback than others. You may do all the training, or it may be split among a group, letting the student meet people from around the library and learn who is the expert on different subjects. It's a good idea to split training over several days. Remember how you give patrons just the information he can use? That's true in teaching, too. You want to give your student what he can practice in the near future so that you can reinforce good habits and correct bad ones.

That may sound like a lot of time and work, but it doesn't have to be. Here's a good example:

> Bob, we shelve our books in call number order. While you probably know that, it will help you help patrons find books if you know how the call numbers are constructed. There's a short tutorial I'd like you to look at, then I'll answer questions, and we'll look at a floor plan that shows how the stacks are laid out. It'll take about 10 minutes. I'll be in my office when you finish.

Total time: 15 minutes. Time you have to be there, five minutes. Easier tasks, like how to answer the phone and forward a call, may take less time and require only verbal instructions; more difficult tasks, like handling a problem patron, will take considerably longer. Don't be tempted to skip a step because of time constraints. Remember the teachable moment? He needs the basic skills first, and luckily those tend to be the easiest to teach. That gives you some time to coordinate teaching the interview.

TRAINING TOOLS

There are many tools you can use for training. There are videos on YouTube and online tutorials like LCEasy. You can put your training materials on Blackboard or another content management system, you can have a wiki, you can have a frequently-asked-question site for students and staff, and you can have all of them or make your own. What is most important is that the student can access them and review them since some tasks will occur only occasionally and are easy to forget.

Role playing is a way to practice tasks that are critical or involve people skills. You can't count on a problem patron when you're ready to teach how to deal with one, and it may be an intimidating situation for your student. It helps to have a third person play the patron since having your boss yell at you is pretty intimidating, too. Your staff or other students can fill that part. You can use scripts or just let them draw on their experiences. Most of us have met Slacker Dude, Miss Very Vague, Mister Big Business, and Old Yeller and can do a variation of the character. Role playing gives the student a safe way to hone his skills.

When he's ready to try those skills for real, he should have someone who can unobtrusively help when needed. He should know the person and feel comfortable asking questions or turning the interview over entirely. You should feel comfortable that that person can discuss the encounter and give your student good feedback on his performance, too.

LESSON 1: HELLO!

If you are a paraprofessional already, you've probably encountered patrons who come to you because you look like you work there or you look like you know what you're doing; people are used to asking people they see in retail stores. You may not be able to answer their question, but you know where to send them. You've already mastered part of the service without even knowing it.

All too often, the librarian is on his computer, reading a new journal, or talking to another person. He looks busy (and he is), but the reference librarian's job is to answer questions for patrons. You need to look like that's what you're there for. You can do that by smiling at the patron, greeting him, and moving around the library looking for people who look like they need help. If the reference desk is slow, you may be tempted to rush the interview and get back to what you were doing, but what you are doing at the desk is helping patrons. You shouldn't get distracted by other things.

Turn so that your body is toward the patron. You want to look the him in the face. You want to make eye contact but not stare into his eyes. You can look between the eyes or at his forehead or look at one eye and shift to the other. This is not easy for many people, especially if you come from a culture where this is considered rude or you're inherently shy. After all, looking someone in the eyes is a very personal and inviting—or challenging—thing to do. Practice on other staff, your friends, and even your pets. You don't want to stare them down; rather, just convey that you see them, that you're interested in helping them, and that you are initiating the encounter. Avoid gestures that distract the patron and ignore the patron's gestures that may seem out of place.

Try to be at the patron's level, so if you're working with a child, sit down. If you're at a desk, you may want to stand. Being at the same general level prevents either of you from feeling intimidated. Standing shows that you are willing to move to help the patron.

LESSON 2: HOW CAN I HELP YOU?

Yes, you will feel like a retail clerk. That's because retail has been doing it and studying how to welcome people and help them for a long time. They know what they're doing, and you should, too.

You don't have to have a pat line that you use every time. In fact, you shouldn't; rather, you should sound like you're encountering a patron for the first time. What you definitely don't want to sound is bored. Here are a few opening lines you can use (or make up your own):

- Are you finding what you need?
- How's it going? Do you need any help?
- Good morning! Can I help you find something?
- What can I help you with today?

You want to establish a relationship, even if it is temporary. You want to look and sound like a nice, helpful person. Part of that is giving the patron your whole attention. Put down anything in your hands. Don't look at your monitor. You might want to cock your head to one side slightly, not unlike your dog does when you talk to him. That's a sign of interest. Nonverbal cues are very important in looking welcoming and friendly.

LESSON 3: THE BIG QUESTION

It doesn't matter what the question is, you will start the same way. The patron will state his question, and you will listen. That sounds easy enough, but you want to be an active listener. Acknowledge the question, let him finish talking, and then clarify it. Some patrons will know exactly what they want, but most won't. They have an idea of what it is but don't know exactly how to ask, where it would be, or what section it would live in. You want to encourage them to give you all the details they can. Nod, smile, and say "Uh-huh" or "Okay." When they stop, you can chime in.

Encourage the patron to give you more details if you need them. Once you think you have the whole question, paraphrase it and repeat it. That gives the patron a chance to elaborate more or to give a yes-or-no answer.

Some patrons ask easy factual questions that can be answered by books in your ready-reference section. At that point, you can jump to the closing. If not, keep going.

What needs to clarified or expanded on? Don't just ask; tell them why you're asking. "I don't want to repeat what you've already done. Have you looked in the catalog for a book?" Just asking "Have you looked in the catalog?" is insulting to someone who has been trying to find something unsuccessfully.

Other phrases include the following:

- What would be the perfect thing to find?
- I'm not sure I know what that is. Can you tell me more?
- What particular part of the subject are you interested in?
- How do you need the information? Will a website work for you?

Think of the classic questions a reporter asks: what, where, who, how, when? You now know what; next comes the rest. Does the patron need it right now, or do you have time for an interlibrary loan? Is it for the patron or for his mother? "Okay, do you want a book, or will an article work?" How recent does the information have to be? What level of information is needed: fifth grade, professional, or consumer? How much information does he need: a paragraph, several articles for a paper, or books for a thesis?

When you ask about a deadline, phrase it that way. If you ask when the patron needs it, the answer will always be "Now." The answer to that is "We always get the information as soon as possible; when is the last date you can use it?"

Don't forget to ask about the "how": people see libraries filled with books and often don't know about the other media we have. As time goes on, more and more of our information is not on paper, but patrons may not realize that there is online information that isn't available on the open Web or that it may be on microfilm.

Verify the spelling of names, places, and unknown words. Even if you think you know, you may be wrong. Is the patron asking for a book on Freud interested in Sigmund or his grandson, artist Lucian? Getting paint off bear skin or bare skin? The Lion King the movie, the musical, the cast album, or the book? You may know what 90 percent of your patrons are looking for, but this may be one of the 10 percent you don't. Don't assume that you know what the patrons want: ask.

Don't get ahead of yourself. Be sure to rephrase the question and ask if you have it right. If the patron adds more details or says "No, I really need this instead," go back and start again. It happens.

LESSON 4: THE POSSIBLE ANSWERS

Don't forget what you've learned already. If the patron hasn't looked in the online public access catalog (OPAC), let him watch you search and talk as you're doing it. If the patron seems interested, you can offer to teach him more about doing it. You glance up at him as you read things you've found so that you can read his nonverbal cues. It's likely you'll find several sources. Don't just write down the call numbers; that's not much help for nonlibrarians. Include the title. If the answer is from a database or the OPAC, offer to e-mail it to the patron or print it off.

Sometimes it's a good news/bad news situation. Sandwich the bad in with the good: "There is an answer, but it's not here. I can get it by interlibrary loan if you like" or "I can't get it in that time frame. I can give you who to contact directly, though."

Avoid jargon or explain it. This is the point at which paraprofessionals excel: they can empathize with the patrons as someone who doesn't speak librarianese. It's also good practice for librarians since patrons won't learn to speak our language, and there is no reason for them to.

"Would you like me to look it up for you or show you how?" We'd prefer to teach, but patrons may not care, may never look up that category again, may not have time, and may not retain it if you do teach them. One compromise is to let the patron watch you search and talk while doing it. It's teaching by example, which is a good teaching method. Your library may have a policy on teaching or not; the tendency is for academic libraries to teach and public ones not to, but there are exceptions and differences everywhere, even within the same library.

However, you should know how to create a search strategy. Where will you look first? What if you don't know anything about the subject? Neither of you know how to spell a term? The general rule is to go from general to specific. A quick Google search will give you an idea of what field it's in, so you can go to an encyclopedia or dictionary. With that information in hand, you can go to an index or database or your OPAC. Spending some time in the tutorials for databases will pay off now since you'll know where to go first. If a key word turns up too much, try a Boolean search or refine your question. If it doesn't turn up anything at all, try it again elsewhere.

Explaining how you arrived at your search strategy and how you use it gives the patron a chance to learn and you a chance to keep the conversation going. The awkward pause while you search can feel very long for the patron, and you want to include him in your search. You are partners, after all, in looking for the information. He establishes the question, and you help find the information.

One of the fun things to do is to share "librarian magic." Most people don't know what the list of terms at the side of a database or OPAC is or how to use them. When you teach a session, have a fairly futile search that gives you just one or two results and then click one of the formal terms and tell them that it will magically give them all the related results. It perks up a class that's getting dull, and the students will remember it as that cool thing the librarian taught them. We can use a little cool in our reputations.

When a patron tells you what he searched for, don't take him at his word; rather, try some other terms. Patrons don't always remember to write things down or exactly what they searched for the last time. When you search, try synonyms and related terms or look at the Library of Congress headings. If you find an answer that's close, look at the terms and choose the one that fits. Then you can check what other terms are used in the items you find that way.

For the paraprofessional (as well as the new librarian), the hardest thing is often to say "I don't know." Get over it. Sure, it could make you look dumb, so practice saying it in a way that makes you look like you're giving exceptional customer service and makes you feel good: "What a good question! Let me get someone who specializes in those" or "Let me start you with this, and I'll send in an expert in the subject while you're working." You can explain that you're not a librarian or that you're new; the job is to get the best service for the patron. Paraprofessionals should know your limits and know when to refer to a librarian. Never misrepresent yourself as a librarian. You may have special knowledge, however, that will serve the patron well. You may empathize with being lost in the stacks, know better ways to explain jargon, and know the software better than the librarians. They may often call on you for help.

LESSON 5: THE CLOSING

When you think you've got it covered, take another tip from retail and let the patron know he's welcome to come back for more. It also gives the patron a chance to say "I was really looking for something else." It also gives the patron a clue that you're finished. You'll want that when you get the chatty patron who wants to show you pictures of his grandkids: "If you need more help, I'll be here until four. If it's after that, tell the person here you talked to Jane" or "Is there anything else I can help with?"

You can close the interview too early if you start getting bored, you think the patron is repeating himself, or you just think you've spent enough time with that patron. You can let it go too long if you think the patron is attractive or interesting. You may think that you're hiding either impression, but it's not likely that you are. In either case, use one of your closing statements to find out if the patron has enough information and close the interview.

Sometimes the patron will end the interview before you think you're done. That may mean that you've given enough information for him, that he doesn't think you're helping, or that he now has enough information to go forward on his own. He might just find you annoying or be having a bad day. Patrons are usually too polite to say "You're not getting it," but if he's giving clues that he's done, you want to close the interview with an invitation to come back in any case.

Another tip from retail is to never let the customer leave empty handed. In a library, that may be figurative, but if you can't answer a question, give a referral to another library, repository, or agency that may be able to help him. Offer to call ahead and tell them what he's looking for, to save time, or to e-mail them and have them get in touch with the patron.

A checklist to cover all the facets of the job, from introductions to their boss to skills and tasks that are expected, can keep everyone on track and make sure that no one assumes that someone else covered it. It also lets the new person see what he can expect from his training.

There are several ways to train, and you should try all of them because you'll learn something different each time. Observation is a very passive way and has to be done with someone who is willing to talk about what he's doing and why. After a session or two, take the chair and let the other librarians observe you. It's vital that the trainee get lots of feedback, mostly positive: "You found out the details well; if you hadn't asked when he needed it, he would have been still waiting for an interlibrary loan" or "I liked the way you turned your monitor around, but you might have explained more—he seemed to be following you."

You can also get feedback from videos with the patron's permission. That gives you a way to observe yourself and how you handle a transaction. With inexpensive cameras and cell phone video, it's easier to do and less obvious than in years past with large video cameras. If people shy away from that, there are samples on YouTube of both good and purposely bad interviews.

Role playing is another way. It's hard for someone who works in the library to pretend that they don't know anything about it, so volunteers who have acting skills or who are students can take the patron role. There are a number of scripts online, or you can write your own using common questions and situations.

A hundred years ago or so, there were only two ways to have a reference interview: in person or by phone or perhaps by mail. Now there are many—most never heard of 40 years ago. Although the principles of the reference interview remain the same, you also want to train your new staff to do phone, e-mail, chat, and whatever else he is responsible for. He'll need to practice those with feedback, too.

Here's a checklist you can use, every day, to make sure you are giving good service to your patrons:

Greet the patron, smile, and make eye contact

Acknowledge patron statements and encourage him to elaborate. Ask open questions and for clarification

Repeat the question in your own words

Look for the answer, include the patron in your search, and refer to another librarian or source if necessary

Ask if you've answered his question and whether he has any more questions-enCourage patron to return

---

A little GARLAC will spice up the interview and make it come out just right.

Patrons will expect you to help them in more ways than we are sometimes prepared to. Your library will have rules in place, no doubt, for who is responsible for changing a toner cartridge. Who is responsible for access problems with an online source: you or the information technology department? How does the patron know, and why should he care? You will be regarded as the face of the library.

You should know some things just by your experience, but some things are not taught in library science programs, even today. In part, that is because every library has either different tools or different staffing models. In a one-person library, you may be the information technology department, while a large library may have its own department.

As a new reference librarian in your library or a paraprofessional, you will have to start from scratch or near it. Part of training for new staff should include who to refer technical problems to and how to handle the ones you are responsible for. A large part of that is personal skills: how to communicate the problem and offer alternates. Someone is printing off a thousand pages and the patron has two that he needs printed right now? Can you have him e-mail them to you and print them from your office? Is there another computer center with a printer?

A reference wiki is a great place for you to store what you're learning and to pass on information picked up during a shift. Did 10 people come in looking for a map of the city in 1893? That's a good clue that it's homework or a group project; you can list the sources you found for the next patron. Who do you call about a certain problem? That's a good list to save. It's also a good place for listing resources: subject guides or pathfinders (which can easily be updated), ready-reference sources, subject encyclopedias, indexes, and subject bibliographies.

Make sure that your new staff have a chance to practice with the software for chat and other services. Make sure that they have someone who can help with problems, as anxiety happens on both sides of the reference desk. That can be with an assigned mentor or a rotating schedule that lets them work with everyone.

Give people time to practice the reference interview itself. It's not an intuitive thing. Most of us think that people will ask for what they need and take some time to get used to the idea that they don't know what to ask for.

Teach people how to pass questions from one shift to the next. A form, whether paper or online, is a good way to be sure you have all the information they need:

- Name
- Affiliation (are they one of your patrons)
- Contact information
- Best time to be reached (if by phone)
- Topic
- Format needed
- When needed
- Sources checked
- Your name

They should know how to pass questions as referrals, too. Call ahead so that you know the person will be there and let him know who is coming and all the information that you've gathered. By doing that, you can save the time of both the patron and the librarian. Everyone needs to know when to refer a patron, or quality will suffer. It's the difference between seeing a nurse and a doctor: both are competent, but one's an expert.

You can use chat transcripts, with identifying information removed, to review with your staff. The secret is to use both good and bad sessions so that someone can see the difference. After the first review, pick a different group of good sessions and let people point out the good ways a question is handled.

There are tools for many of the training tasks. LCEasy is already there, so there's no need to reinvent the wheel. Your online information literacy tutorials can help both staff and librarians learn what databases you have and how they are used. New staff need some time to look at the tutorials in the databases and do some searching.

Brown-bag lunches are a great way for people to connect and to exchange experiences. You can pick a topic to talk about or let one come up from people's experiences. Someone should be a "leader" to make introductions and keep things moving. Peer-to-peer learning is a relief from the checklist-and-class routine of training. So does coffee with a mentor, a time for one-on-one questions and comments.

Paraprofessionals, students, and volunteers have probably not dealt with confidentiality issues before, and their importance needs to be stressed. They need to be taught that every part of the interview is confidential and that some questions need a private place to be discussed. That may be the point to hand off to a librarian, although that should be determined in each library.

Finally, give your new staff feedback often, even weekly. Evaluation is meant to help them improve; if it's given only annually, it doesn't help them. It doesn't have to be a formal procedure and should include a chance for the new employee to ask questions and make suggestions. After all, a new employee is a fresh set of eyes who can point out things that you're so used to that they are routine. Make your suggestions constructive ones: "Bob, you found just what she was looking for! Good job. You might want to tell her what you're doing when you're searching, though, so she has some input" or "That patron was very difficult to satisfy, wasn't she? Nothing you said or did was good enough for her. She would have been a good one to turn over to a librarian."

ONLINE TOOLS FOR TEACHING

If you work in a large library or have frequent turnover, you may find yourself teaching the reference interview over and over again. That can be very time consuming, and the people you need to teach other parts may not be available when you need them. They may not be available when the student needs to review something. Worst of all, your best reference librarian may move or retire, and all that experience may be lost.

It doesn't have to be. You can create your own teaching tools with little cost and little experience. Before you do, make sure that no one else has done what you need. YouTube and other library sites are good places to check before you make your own. Library students often make videos for their classes and portfolios. General tasks, like welcoming behaviors, apply to any reference service. Others, like specific collections and policies, you can do yourself.

Wikis are probably the easiest thing you can do. "Wiki" means "quick" in Hawaiian, and wikis are fast websites that need no programming knowledge. There are a number of hosted sites that you can use, or you can install software on your own server. Both come in open and password-protected versions. You can install it behind your firewall, where it is available to your staff but not the general public.

Wikis let anyone with access add or edit information. Anyone can add pages. No one needs to know any programming. They're usually self-formatting. It doesn't get much simpler than that.

Wikipedia is probably the best known wiki, but yours doesn't have to be that big. Divide it into sections that are useful. The reference interview, reference sources, homework assignments, referral sources, and policies will give your staff a central place to go for information.

The hardest part of starting a wiki is adding the initial information that makes it useful. You will have to get staff buy-in for the start-up and updating. There is some investment in training and start-up, but since the software is free, this will be in staff time.

Students are used to wikis, and you can often have them or staff members enter data from old notebooks and index cards. They will often have ideas for what should be included, too.

Blogs, or Web logs, are a simple way to post things to the Internet and let people pose or answer questions. They are usually used as journals or to post announcements, but they can be used to truly collaborate on answering questions. You can use one to share your training materials and experiences with other libraries. You can use RSS feeds to send them to your reader so that you don't have to check them all, and you should have an RSS button on yours, too.

There are many hosted blog sites, and none need programming experience. You can usually choose a visual scheme, or you can program one to match your site. Be sure to explain what its purpose is and who you are so that outside users can evaluate it in those terms.

Unless your blog is behind a firewall, you'll likely want to approve posts so that you don't have spam problems. That means that someone will have to check in and approve them, but that's not a large time expenditure.

You can repurpose what you write for your blog to a social networking site. You can use it to publicize events. You can use it internally for training and updates for your staff. You can also use it to capture the collective wisdom of your staff. Once you have something in writing, you can copy it to your wiki with no further effort. Repurposing content in any media saves time and broadens your outreach.

Podcasts are audio or video broadcasts that are downloadable and playable on computers or personal mobile devices. Audio podcasts can give step by step directions for a task while the learner is doing it; shorter podcasts can give directions for a smaller part of a task. Both have advantages, and it's easy to break a long podcast into shorter ones that the learner can refer to without repeating the whole podcast. There are a number of free audio editors available to use, and you can edit out pauses and background noises. It's simple to record a live presentation and upload it as a podcast.

Video podcasts are most famous as YouTube. You can make them with a cell phone camera, but they are just as easy, if not easier, using an inexpensive video recorder. Editing is a little more technical, but not outside the skills of a tech-savvy librarian. You can record a whole instructional session and use it over and over, so it's well worth a little time spent in recording and uploading it or just burning it to CD or DVD for individual use.

Videos can let you record a practice session of a skill and let the student review it and evaluate it later. You can record role-playing sessions or record a student's body language and let him see himself as others do.

Podcasts are a good way to teach your patrons new skills, too. You'll want to make them more general, like how to find job ads or how to use the catalog. Any tasks that you teach patrons repeatedly are good topics. You can also record them in multiple languages so that you can orient new patrons to the library or tell them about special services. Publicize them on Facebook and link them on your front page and have the URLs featured on your screensaver.

Screencasts are similar to pushing screens during a chat reference session. You can record practice sessions in virtual reference or tutorials for database search-ing. The learner can pause it or rewind it to clarify points that might be missed. Screencasts can have audio tracks recorded as they are made or added later. They allow you to demonstrate what and where you are clicking on your screen and what the results are. Unlike cobrowsing, the student can only watch and not interact, but they are good methods for teaching specific skills.

This is another media where you can use the skills you learn to make screen-casts for your patrons, too. Demonstrating how to use an online database or your OPAC can be broken into usable bites that can be reviewed whenever the patron needs to.

Interactive tutorials can be as simple or complicated as you make them. You can use animation and Java, but you can use plain vanilla HTML as well. You can also integrate media with them.

For example, you can have a video clip of an interview, then go to a page that asks you to answer questions. If you answer incorrectly, you go to a page that says, "Sorry, that's incorrect. He should have asked what age level was needed. Try again!," with a "back" button. If you answer correctly, it says, "Very good! You spotted the mistake," and has a "next" button. This type of interactive tutorial corrects mistakes and reinforces correct answers and lets the user go back and review the video.

The advantages of this type of tutorial are that they let the learner review his work and the materials and that they are not timed. The learner can take his time and really assimilate what he's seeing. They also take very little time to create and little technical knowledge. They can be done with any number of programs or coded by hand with a cheat sheet to refer to.

Mashups refer to a blending of materials, often software. If you use different systems for instant messaging and e-mail but use another piece of software to merge them into one interface, you made a mashup. That's not as simple as it sounds, but not too difficult if you have an information technology department or a little programming experience. You can develop your own system using free-ware and a little talent. There are also mashups available from other libraries; if you search, you'll find them mentioned in blogs and journal articles.

Freeware is open source software that you can download, use, and alter as you wish. Major repositories of freeware include http://sourceforge.net and http://www.tucows.com. They also have shareware, which are demo products or free trials.

Some of the useful freeware include Audacity, an audio recorder and editor, and Wordpress for blogging. Google also offers platform-independent software for blogging, wikis, and photo editing. The Library Success wiki has a list of open-source software for libraries, including OPACs. These are Web-based programs, so there's nothing to download and install, but you can lose your access if your account is hacked into. Both Windows and Mac computers have built-in software, like Windows Movie Maker and iMovie for Macintosh. You can find other programs and tutorials all over the Web, so cost need not be a factor. However, time will be a factor, as there is a learning curve for all these programs, but most are easy to use.

You can share your materials on WebJunction, the Online Computer Library Center site. Handouts, screencasts, webinars, and podcasts can be uploaded to share or downloaded to use. This site is aimed at staff and public libraries for the most part, but there are sections for many other topics useful for other types of libraries.

Checklist for Orientation and Training

Introduce the employee to staff and supervisors

Tour of the library and explain hours and functions of departments

Review emergency procedures for both staff and patron issues—problem patrons, weather, and injuries

Staffing issues—when to take breaks and who will cover break time, calling in sick, and so on

Go over policies—confidentiality, priorities, limits to services, when to refer patrons to a librarian, and how to handle complaints

Go over related activities—keeping statistics, filing, and tracking distance reference questions

Review duties

Review resources for staff—departmental wiki, frequently-asked-questions site, and ready-reference collection

Specific skills:

Using the OPAC

Using databases—their strengths and weaknesses

Answering the phone and taking messages and forwarding calls

Using subject headings and reading call numbers

Placing holds and reserves

Using readers' advisory tools and sites

Search strategies

Conducting the reference interview

Observation time

Practice time

OPEN AND CLARIFYING QUESTIONS

- When you say X, do you mean more like Y than Z?
- I'm not sure I know what you mean when you say X. Can you explain it to me?
- Can you give me more details about X?
- Can you give me an example of X?
- What kind of information do you need about X?
- The most current statistics are from 2001. Is that recent enough?
- How much information do you need on the subject?
- I'm not familiar with that person. What is she known for?
- What has stopped you at this point?

Sample Interviews

I need a book about sex.

What do you want to know about it?

Oh, I know all about it. I need something for kids.

What age-group are you looking for? Teens or something younger?

Not teens, really, like a 10-year-old.

All right, do you want fiction or something factual?

Facts! Do they write sex stories for kids? That's sick!

There are stories where the kids are going through puberty and talk about the changes they're going through. But you want something more factual?

Yeah, something about puberty, but it has to be facts and not what she's hearing about at school.

Okay, you need something about girls going through puberty, for a younger girl. Let's see what's in the catalog.

I need a good book about gardening.

All right, do you want something about flowers and vegetables? Or something that's more general?

Well, I'm from Arizona, so I don't really know what you can grow around here. I guess I need to know how to choose vegetables that will grow here. We can't grow anything back home.

All right, there are some good books on growing vegetables in the region. The state agricultural service has some good websites about growing in the state, too, and you can write them for free information booklets. I'll give you their URL for later, and then we can look at the books we have here.

Do you have any good romances?

We have a lot of them. What kind of romance are you looking for?

Not one of those drugstore things, something better than that.

Can you tell me about one that you've enjoyed?

I can't remember the name, but it was about a woman who lived in the Midwest and her friends. They all had all these issues, you know, but they worked them out.

Were they issues with men or just in general?

Well, both. They had pretty bland lives, but one was shy, one was homely, one was divorced, then they each met a guy who kind of spiced life up, but they all stayed in the town at the end. I liked that.

What was it about it you liked?

It wasn't about rich and famous women; they were just friends living normal lives in the middle of nowhere, but they found romance anyways. Not with guys who were rich and famous, either, but they were just good guys. It was real life, but there was romance, too.

Okay, let's take a look at what we have in our reading lists. We have lists of a lot of categories within romances; they're pretty popular. Here's one for books set in small towns and the country, here's one where there are groups of friends, and here's one about everyday people who find love. Why don't you take copies of each and look around? If you read the book jackets, they'll tell you what they're about in more detail.

Okay, I'll do that. There's just so many of them I don't know where to start.

Well, this will give you a starting point. If you like any of them, let me know the next time you're here, and we can look for more from the list. Or maybe find something new. There are some lists online, too, if you want to check them.

ROLE PLAYING

The trainer or another employee plays the role that is defined, and the student interviews him to find out the real information need and suggest resources that are available locally.

The Questioning Teen

A young man wonders if he is gay since he's never kissed a girl or gone on a date. He can't talk to his friends or family about it, but he doesn't know who else to ask. He's very embarrassed to ask for information.

His opening question: "Where are your sex books?"

The Helicopter Parent

A woman has a 17-year-old son who is learning disabled and reads at a fifth-grade level. She wants him to join the debate team because it will look good on his record for college applications. She wants him to read everything on the topic this year: "Should the drinking age be lowered to allow legal adults to drink?"

Her opening question: "Where are your law books? I need to check them all out."

The Sandwich Daughter

A divorced woman has three children at home and one in college nearby. Her mother has had a stroke and cannot live on her own, and she is considering bringing her to live at her home for the near future while she recovers. She needs to find out what resources there are to support her mother's recovery and what effect it will have on her children. She also wonders if her college-aged daughter can help care for her without endangering her grades.

Her opening question: "Where are the books about strokes and children?"

The Family Historian

An older woman is researching her family tree and is interested in finding family records that may be related. She brings a large notebook full of charts and photocopies that she is willing to share with you. She suspects that her great-great aunt was institutionalized in your town since there was a county home for the insane, and this is the last town she sent a letter from.

Her opening question: "I'm looking for Susan Smith. Her married name was Jones, she married John Jones in 1834 in Ohio, in Big County. Her sister Sarah was never married; she was born in 1835. They all started moving west about 1856, and I can find Susan in Missouri, but I can't find anything about Sarah, so I thought I'd check here in Indiana since we're here. Where are the mental hospital records at? Do you have birth certificates filed by last name?"

The Preschooler

A young child wants a book that her friend liked. She can't remember what it's called, but it has a cat in a big hat and it's by a doctor.

Her opening question: "Where are the doctor books? Are they by the cat books?"

The High School Student

A teenager needs three sources of criticism on *Moby Dick*. He hasn't read the book yet, but the paper is due in three days. He has the assignment in his backpack.

His opening question: "Do you have *Moby Dick* on DVD? Or a graphic novel? And I need some short articles on it, too. Some criticism, you know?"

The Movie Fan

An older man wants to see the movie he took his wife to on their first date. Their fiftieth anniversary is in three weeks, and he remembers that it was about a man and an unmarried mother and starred Cary Grant.

His opening question: "Do you have Cary Grant movies?"

The Easy Reader

A woman wants something to read while she's recovering from wrist surgery. She likes books that concern animals but not necessarily about animals. She likes female characters who are strong and self-reliant and who have strong friendships but not romantic ones. It shouldn't be too intricate, just something that will pass the time in the hospital and at home. She wants several books, in large print, since she is very nearsighted.

Her opening question: "Where are your large books?"

The Author

An author is writing a novel about a terrorist plot to assemble a dirty bomb on a train and leave it in a Midwest train station. They build the bomb out of nuclear medical waste, but he doesn't know where they get it or how much it would take. He needs technical details to make it believable.

His opening question: "I need to find where they dispose of nuclear medical waste, what the elements are, how much is disposed of each year, and what it would take to destroy a city the size of, oh, Kansas City. How big is Kansas City?"

The Doctor

A doctor has a patient with an aggressive but unknown infection. The patient has been in the tropics lately but wasn't ill until a few weeks later. He faces amputation of his legs unless the infection can be identified and treated in the next few hours.

His opening question: "I need everything you have on tropical pathogens and vectors, and I need it now. Right now."

REFERENCE

Havighurst, Robert James. *Human Development and Education*. New York: Longmans, Green, 1952.

FURTHER READING

Caufield, James. "Tricky Devil: A Humorous Training Technique for the Chat Reference Environment." *The Electronic Library* 23, no. 4 (2005): 377–82.

Connell, R. S., and P. J. Mileham. "Student Assistant Training in a Small Academic Library." *Public Services Quarterly* 2, no. 2 (2006): 69–84.

Faix, Allison I., Margaret H. Bates, Lisa A. Hartman, Jennifer H. Hughes, Casey N. Schacher, Brooke J. Elliot, and Alexander D. Woods. "Peer Reference Redefined: New Uses for Undergraduate Students." *Reference Services Review* 38, no. 1 (2010): 90–107.

Gardner, Susan. "Tiered Reference: The New Landscape of the Frontlines." *Electronic Journal of Academic and Special Librarianship* 7, no. 3 (Winter 2006). http://southernlibrarianship.icaap.org/content/v07n03/gardner_s01.htm (accessed June 21, 2010).

Kalvee, Debbie. "Successful Reference Training on a Shoestring." *Library Administration and Management* 10, no. 4 (1996): 210–13.

Kent, Allen. "Closing the Reference Interview." *RQ* 31 (Summer 1992): 503–23.

Library Success. "Open Source Software" (wiki). http://www.libsuccess.org/index.php?title=Open_Source_Software.

McDaniel, Julie Ann. *Training Paraprofessionals for Reference Service: A How-to-Do-It Manual for Librarians*. New York: Neal-Schuman, 1993.

Neuhaus, C. "Flexibility and Feedback: A New Approach to Ongoing Training for Reference Student Assistants." *Reference Services Review* 29, no. 2 (2002): 53–64.

Piaget, Jean. "Cognitive Development in Children: Development and Learning." *Journal of Research in Science Teaching* 2, no. 2 (1964): 176–86.

Pomerantz, Jeffrey, Scott Nicholson, and R. David Lankes. "Digital Reference Triage: Factors Influencing Question Routing and Assignment." *Library Quarterly* 73, no. 2 (April 2003): 103–20.

Sisselman, Peggy. "Exploiting the Social Style of Patrons to Improve Their Satisfaction with the Reference Interview." *Library Review* 58, no. 2 (2009): 124–33.

Whisner, Mary. *Practicing Reference: Thoughts for Librarians and Legal Researchers*. AALL Publications Series No. 73. Buffalo NY: Hein, 2006. A compilation of essays published in *Law Library Journal*.

Whisner, Mary. "Teaching the Art of the Reference Interview." *Law Library Journal* 94, no. 1 (2002): 161–66.

Wu, Q. "Win-Win Strategy for the Employment of Reference Graduate Assistants in Academic Libraries." *Reference Services Review* 31, no. 2 (2003): 141–53.

10 SPECIAL LIBRARIES—LAW, MEDICAL, CORPORATE, PRIVATE, AND ARCHIVES

SPECIAL COLLECTIONS

"Special collections" is the umbrella term used for rare and unique collections. They may include archival materials, rare books, manuscript collections, media collections, and others. The unifying purpose of special collections is to preserve the rare materials, including special storage conditions, special handling procedures, and limited access. They may also hold collections that are rare for other reasons. It may be a collection of every edition of Mark Twain whether a single book is rare or not; the research value is in the comprehensiveness of the collection. Special collections often hold books that are not particularly rare but that are fragile and require special handling.

ARCHIVES

The reference interview in archives is much more extensive than at the reference desk of the library. Part of that is due to the tradition of original order: that the patron may gain insights and information from context that isn't explicitly there. The archivist is less likely to hand you one document and say, "This is it." It is far more common to be given a box to go through yourself. Patrons rarely realize that archives aren't cataloged at the item level, and they will need to spend some—and maybe a lot—of time doing the work themselves.

A few patrons will come to the archive knowing the collection they want and even the box or folder. That's due to the computer age; collections may listed in the catalog, or the finding aids may be online. Finding aids are the archival equivalent of a catalog record; they list the creator of the collection, the dates that are covered, and the contents. Finding aids are no more "the collection" than a book index is "the book." Finding aids index at the collection, box, and folder levels. Many of your patrons won't realize that they will have to do the research themselves—that they cannot simply give a name and get a family history or an address and get a history of the building.

Most people, even faculty and PhDs, have never researched in an archive. There are few information literacy classes for freshmen that cover it. It's not uncommon for a member of an organization or business whose records you hold to come in and ask for "his" records and expect to go through them the way he did in the office. The concept of closed stacks is almost unknown in the United States with its many public libraries.

You will use all the skills you know from the usual reference interview, plus many more that you will learn through reading, observation, and training. In particular, you will have to learn both the collections and their structure and to accept the fact that researchers, especially historians, don't know what they are looking for. Literally. They are searching for clues and references, the pieces they will use in their work rather than any known item.

Archives are not like libraries other than the fact that they hold information. Archives hold information that is unique. That may include manuscript collections, institutional records, business records, local government records, collections of personal or political papers, or research collections. Some institutions, especially academic ones, separate institutional records from others. Archives of companies or private institutions may not be open to outside researchers or may have very different rules.

Archives are organized differently than libraries, too. Archives rely on the principle of original order: that the way a collection is structured tells you about the creator. Except for digitized items or items of exceptional value, either for research or intrinsically, they are rarely cataloged at the item level. They may be cataloged at the collection level (Jones photographs, 1 box), series. (Smith family papers, correspondence, boxes 3–5), or folder level (Brown Papers, birth records, box 3, folder 5). The detail of the record is based on the real or anticipated use of the collection. However, collections may have been processed decades ago and may not have anticipated modern uses. In fact, the papers least likely to have been processed back then may be the most used today. The history of women, the poor, and ethnic groups may exist in collections but may not have been valued back then, so it remains buried.

Archives also may have limits to accessibility. Unlike books in a library, an archive may have donor restrictions that close them to researchers for a specific time periods. Some records may be closed by law, like personnel or health records. The records are preserved because of their rarity and are often fragile, requiring patrons to use surrogates, such as photocopies or microfilm.

It's always good to give patrons as much information as possible before they come since many researchers will not be from your institution. Have them on your website, have brochures around the building and at other archives and libraries, and hand them out at conventions. A simple three-fold photocopy is cheap, prepares your patrons for what they'll encounter, and is a good way to get your name out there.

The reference interview in archives usually starts when you come in the door since you'll have to explain all the rules and procedures. If you have a little time and a little talent (or a talented student), you can do a podcast or webcast to explain them. Don't expect all the patrons to see them before they come, but you can let them watch on a computer and replay as much as they want.

Greet the patron. You'll have to stand to make a copy of his ID, so you're going to stand anyways, and this makes you look alert and friendly.

It may be helpful to have a copy of the finding aids or collection descriptions at the desk if they're not online and the patron hasn't seen them. That might save you time if the patron has heard that you have Lincoln's baby photos. Once you've established that you have materials that the patron might want to use, have him fill in a registration form. Explain that the form isn't used by your development office or anyone else but is part of your security routine. He should sign a copy of your rules sheet, and you should have extra copies for patrons to use in the reading room. They should sign your logbook if you have one. Part of registration could be a photocopy of an ID. Check it to see that the names and numbers match. Some archives require the ID to be left at the desk, but you'll want to check with your legal counsel. Modern student IDs often have a credit chip embedded, and this raises other security questions. Explain that the registration has to be done only once and that thereafter he can show his ID and sign the logbook while you add the new date to his registration form.

Explain what materials can be taken into the reading room and what's already there. You should have lockers or another secure area for patrons to leave their belongings; most are leery of turning their briefcase or purse over to you to hold behind your desk. Explain your policy on photocopying and digital photography, which should be on your rules sheet, too.

Now you're ready to start the reference interview itself. The first thing you want to explain is how different archives are from libraries, that you have different rules because of the unique items, and that you'll be glad to help at any point. You should be in or go into the reading room frequently to see how the patron is doing and ask if the materials are helping him. Ask the patron about his interests and if there's a specific collection he wants to use. The patron may be vague; many researchers in the humanities are looking for leads, not known items. You should have a good idea from his registration form, but you can add notes to it as you talk. Explain how your archives works: Does the patron fill out a call slip, or do you? How long of a wait will it be to get materials to him? Where materials are stored, be it in several places or even in a remote facility, may be significant. How much material do you allow in the reading room, and how much can you hold while he's working? Can you hold boxes until the next day if he's coming back?

Explain your finding aids, catalogs, and services. If you require that microfilm be used and the original brought only when it's necessary to see it personally, explain that. Remind patrons to keep materials in the order in which they are found and that they should put papers away each time they leave the reading room. Explain that he should use one folder or box at a time and then replace it to maintain original order. Show him how to use an acid-free paper bookmark to mark things he wants copied or how to fill out a copy request form and whether you can make copies while he waits or if he will have to return for them. Explain how to use reference slips, which should have a place for the patron's name and signature.

Ideally, there should be two staff members so that one can retrieve materials while the other supervises the patrons. One staff member can be on call until needed to retrieve materials or make photocopies if you're a small archive.

Check each box for collation and completeness before and after the patron uses it. Each time the patron leaves the reading room, inspect any personal materials that were allowed into the room. That may be awkward, so you should explain that you'll do that early in the interview.

In a situation where constant supervision cannot be provided, it is crucial to check patrons' belongings when they exit the room or building. This can be awkward, too, but it will be easier if the procedures and the reasons for them are clearly explained to patrons at the outset.

It is also important to have policies and training to deal with difficult situations. What should you do if a patron refuses to provide registration information or refuses to have his belongings inspected? What should you do if a patron mishandles collections while working with them? (Brown and Patkus 2010)

Your form should include the following:

- Name
- Local address
- Permanent address
- Phone
- E-mail
- Research interest and enough space to go into detail
- ID type and numbers
- Dates, with enough space for return visitors' dates
- Affiliation (faculty, student, member, public)
- For publication? (you may have other forms to give him or have him sign)
- Collections used (you'll have to keep that updated as he requests more)
- Rules statement (I have received copy of the archives rules and procedures and will comply with them)
- Signature
- Date

RARE BOOKS

Rare books are not always old despite the popular perception. They may include artists' books, limited editions, or books that have associational value, having been owned by a notable person. One book from Einstein's library doesn't tell you much about him, but the full library will.

Rare books often holds book-related collections. These include bookplates, publisher records, or authors' manuscripts.

Rare books usually have special handling requirements and limitations. You will have to explain these to the patrons, too. There may be special cradles for the books so that their spines don't crack. The patron may need to wear gloves in some libraries but not at others. Or they may be required with certain books and not others.

The patron may want to use the book not for its content but for its physical form. There are clues to the history of the volume or its provenance. There are clues that tell them about its publisher and binder or the press it was printed on. You will need to ask about both the volume that the patron is looking for and what he is looking for. Examining the binding or structure of the book can damage the book, so it warrants asking in the reference interview.

Since cell phones with cameras and digital cameras are so common, it's reasonable to limit photocopying of rare books to a minimum. A handout with photography guidelines will be helpful in explaining how the volume can be photographed since patrons often want to prop it up or move it to a place with better lighting to get a good shot. That can be very damaging. Some rare book departments have overhead scanners or their own cameras and do not allow patrons to do the photography themselves. The images can then be e-mailed to the patron or printed out.

MANUSCRIPTS

Manuscripts have special meanings in special collections. They may be what we often think of as manuscripts (the first notes for a book), but they also include other writings and noninstitutional records.

Registration and reference are similar to archives. In fact, they may well share forms and space in the department.

Because patrons may have to travel a great distance to come to your special collections, much more of the initial reference interview is done by phone or e-mail, and many of the answers are given the same way. Policies differ between special collections, so don't assume that if they've used an archive, they know your policies. Some let cameras be used, and some don't; some let you make your own photocopies, and some don't. They also differ by institution. Some keep genealogical information, microfilm, and photocopies in special collections. Some have one copy of a book that circulates, while the other stays in special collections. Some require you to use microfilm if they have it.

Patrons will expect your help for referrals, too. There are print and online directories of other archives and collections, and you should develop some knowledge of local sources. A frequently-asked-questions site, even if just for internal use, can help you refer patrons to a likely source. A list of contacts can speed the process, especially when you can call ahead and explain the patron's question. Be prepared and prepare your patron for the inevitable suggestion that he come and look for himself. Special collections and archives everywhere have the same problems with volume and time to process collections and expect the patron to do his own research. It's a fact of life.

Keep notes on what's available in other formats, online, or on microform. A frequent complaint is that your hours are too short or inconvenient. Having sources that can be checked outside your usual hours can defuse some of the patron's frustration.

GENEALOGY AND LOCAL HISTORY

Genealogists will take a lot of your time if you let them. The phrase "Let me get you started with this . . . " will serve you well. Some researchers are historians and will focus on their search, and some are in the humanities elsewhere and are looking for leads and ideas and will want to see everything and ask your advice about sources. Some are looking for their ancestors and will share every detail about them and where they found it. Not all genealogists are that talkative, but they are searching for their families, something that they might not have been able to do before the collapse of the Soviet Union or the advent of online sources, and are very excited. It's hard to find a more personal subject than family. You will rarely find more enthusiastic and friendlier people.

On the other hand, nothing may be less interesting than someone else's family history. In either case, you have more patrons to help and other things to do, so you can extract yourself gracefully and perform your other duties.

Sources include the U.S. Census, vital records, immigration research, military research, and a variety of other basic genealogy sources. There is an amazing amount of data available online, some fee based and some free, from the Church of Latter-Day Saints and the federal government.

You'll use all the questions you usually do in a reference interview. There are additional questions to ask, too:

- "Is there a specific person or group you're researching?"
- "What do you already know about the subject?"
- "What time period are you looking for?"
- "What brought you to our institution?"

These questions may bring out details that you can use to find resources that the patron never thought of. Sometimes the smallest detail will make you a hero. They may not think that the fact that Grandma went to a particular school is relevant since it burned down long ago, but you may have yearbooks from it. You might know where the papers of a teacher are. Don't be too concerned about sending the patron on a wild goose hunt; that's what genealogists are used to. They make other researchers look uninterested.

You will make a lot of referrals to other repositories and agencies, and having a website or a handout will save both of you a lot of time. Local historical societies, genealogical societies, and city, county, and state archives may all have many more sources than you do. There is sometimes confusion about who has what, and patrons may accuse you of withholding something that a friend says that you do have. In that case, invite the patron to look all he wants but assure him that you do not hide anything. The friend may have seen the item in a book at your repository and not in the collection itself. He might have seen it in the historical society. Offer to call ahead and see what they say and give the patron a map.

This is an area where Google Books can be very helpful since once you have found a name, you can search for it across all the books. Prepare the patron, though, that you can't print many of those resources.

CORPORATE LIBRARIES AND ARCHIVES

In a corporate library, you have only one customer: the corporation. If you can't justify your salary by the service you give, you and the library may be gone. That's scary, but it's also a terrific challenge. Not only will you have to find information for your boss or team at a moment's notice, nut you will have to be proactive and bring new information to the people who can use it. The reference interview is much the same as always, but your results will be dramatically different.

You may give your answer as a written report to the team, as a presentation to the board, or as a database for general use. It may go to the design department, to advertising, or to human resources. The most important and different part of the reference interview in a corporate library is establishing a relationship with your users. You want them to think of you first when they need information and to be available by any and every means they use to communicate.

It will be rare to teach users how to use the resources you have. They hired you to do the research. Unlike other libraries, you will analyze and prepare the information before you give it to the patron. The form that your patron wants will be even more important since it may affect the usefulness of the information.

You will also have to have great time management skills. There will be times you have a number of requests in process and will have to take and prioritize still another one. Tact will come into play here. You will have to establish what the last date (or time) he can use the information is and let him know where he stands in the current work flow. If the patron is the big boss, that may not matter; he may get priority.

There are also cost considerations. The information he needs may be available immediately through an outside vendor but at a considerable cost for the service. Ask the patron if he has a budget that will cover it and be sure that it gets charged to it. Unlike other libraries, each department or project may have its own budget, and you may not want yours charged for their need for speed.

Your reference interview skills will be used to find out what's most useful for your team or boss, and you'll do the work. Having a form that they can complete and send to you to start the process will speed things up considerably, and speed is valuable in the corporate world. Having an online form that the patron can simply fill out and send is helpful, but make sure you get a phone number since a request for immediate information may take a discussion of the options and costs involved. An online form should include the following:

- Your name
- Your professional title/position title
- Your department:
- Your phone (desk and/or cell)
- Your e-mail address
- Deadline (or last date that information can be used)
- Question to be answered. The more information you can give us, the quicker and better we can answer it.
- How will this information be used? This will help us focus on the best format for your answer.
- How current must the information be?
- What do you already know about the topic? You will save time by telling us what is missing from your knowledge.
- What resources, if any, have you already explored?
- If you did an Internet search, what search terms did you use and in what search engine?
- How much information do you need? Will summary-level information be good enough? Do you need data that spans years or a week? How much detail do you need?
- List any special requirements or constraints that we should know about (ProQuest 2010)

SPECIAL LIBRARIES

Special libraries, as opposed to special collections, are focused on a particular field, such as art, law, or medicine. Professional libraries have lots of jargon that people in the profession understand, and you have to understand it, too. A good dictionary in the field will help you and the patron interpret the jargon so that you both understand the question.

Professional libraries, like medical and law libraries, are aimed at one group of specialists. This is a field where you have to know not only what you're doing but also what you can't do. You are not a doctor or a lawyer, you are not licensed, and you cannot give medical or legal advice. You are information professional; you are no more qualified to give advice on law than a lawyer is to give collection development advice. Not only is it unethical, but in most places it is illegal and is treated as unlicensed practice. That is why many law libraries require the librarian to also have a juris doctor degree.

You can refer patrons to other agencies but never to individual practitioners. That would be an endorsement, and that is a job for a professional in that field, not a librarian. You should never give personal experiences or opinions, either. Your job is to provide facts and sources, not to influence the patron.

LAW

Both the law librarian and the reference librarian who get a question on law must walk a fine line between guiding the patron to reliable resources and interpreting them. Legal research often is in particular areas of the law. Laws, regulations, cases, subjects, procedures and location-based instances are the major divisions. You can point patrons in the direction of useful materials, but you should always refer them to a lawyer for advice or information on their personal circumstances.

You can answer directory-type questions, like addresses or phone numbers, or directional ones without any risk. The unlicensed practice of law is a very real issue. The patron who relies on your advice can later sue you, or the bar association can. Every law librarian—or one who may answer questions on law—should read up on what constitutes the unlicensed practice of law.

It's sometimes said that the correct answer to every question in law is "It depends." That's a safe answer to remember when the patron is looking for the "right" answer to a legal question.

If you work in a private law library, your patrons will be the lawyers and staff in the firm. If you work in a public library or a university library, your patrons may be anyone interested in the law or a certain law.

Librarians will do much more teaching than answering questions about the law. You will teach the patron how to research the law and what tools to use. You won't have the time to do that with every patron, so have handouts with the sources and what they cover and how to use them. Have one with the contact information for the bar association, legal aid, courts, and social work agencies. Those are the referrals you can safely make in law. If the patron asks for the name of a lawyer, give him a phone book.

Questions unique to law libraries include the following:

What jurisdiction is needed? International, federal, state, city ordinances?
Do you need the law as passed ("black-letter" law) or case law, where it has been interpreted by the courts? That may change the use of the law.

If the patron has something in print, ask to see it. He may not think the odd letters and numbers are important, but they may actually be a citation to the law he wants. "Title IX" may mean nothing to him, but you can quickly find that it refers to sex discrimination in education.

Law is unique in that not only does it change in each jurisdiction, but the jurisdictions may overlap as well. Federal law applies all over the United States, but local law may not refer to it at all. It doesn't matter; it still applies locally.

How much the patron needs is a major issue. "I need everything on torts" will not help either of you. Even "railroad torts" will not narrow it enough to give effective service. Narrow it down as far as you can with the issue. "Damaged luggage on railroads" may still turn up dozens of cases, but you walk a fine line between finding the law and telling the patron which law he needs.

There are a number of books written to explain different areas of the law in plain language, and they are the first place you should refer a patron to. Legal jargon includes many "terms of art," that don't mean what they sound like. For example, "quiet enjoyment" of your property doesn't mean that your neighbors have to be silent. "Terms of art" are the jargon of law and have nothing to do with the arts. There are a number of good law dictionaries and dictionaries that explain terms in plain English. A guide to abbreviations is also helpful.

There are popular guides written in plain language for common questions. There are books on rental contracts, wills, and even dog law. Courts often have information and handouts on family law and local laws written for the nonlawyer.

One type of patron who is unique to law libraries is the patron who is incarcerated. Those patrons often have a lot of time on their hands and a real interest in the law. They will often contact you by mail or e-mail and ask for advice. Like every other patron, they should get impartial service, but be very careful about giving advice. All should have access to a lawyer and a law library or resources, and you should refer them for any questions concerning their case. That includes questions about the patron's rights and responsibilities. One thing you never want to do is to fill out a form or sign it for the patron since that may commit you to something beyond what's on the paper. Even librarians with juris doctor degrees should avoid them. You can explain that you work for a certain library, and you cannot legally commit to anything on their behalf.

Often a patron will come in with a known-item question but have a partial citation. If you have access to an online service, you can track it down. Otherwise, you may have to start with an encyclopedia or a treatise and try to follow the citations. Google might be of help, but it's less likely than in other fields. Luckily, both law and medicine have specialized indexes and encyclopedias as well as databases.

You can show the patron how to use the index or table of contents of a legal encyclopedia or how to find judicial decisions, legislative acts, and administrative regulations at both the state and the federal level. You can show the patron how to find key words to use in searches of Thomas, the federal laws online, or the Government Printing Office for regulations. You can't tell the patron that a case is one he needs or that it's up to date since the case may have been overruled. That would be advice. Recommending a lawyer is advice, too; you need to recommend them to the bar association or give them a directory to look at.

There are a number of excellent guides to doing legal research both in print and online. They will give the patron most of what he needs to find cases and other sources and explain how to check them for updates and changes. In the interest of information literacy, you will want to tell him that state and federal sites are reliable for finding the law but that other sites and blogs may be prejudiced by the author's experiences or outright solicitation. If the patron is not

Web savvy, you should have a site to send him to or a handout explaining how to evaluate the authority of the sites.

MEDICAL

Just like the legal librarian, the medical librarian is a professional but not a doctor. You know how to find information, but you have little or no training on how to use it correctly. Like the law librarian, you need to know your limits. You can give the patron information but not interpret it, tell the patron what's the treatment, or recommend a doctor. You should never share your experiences, even if you have had the same experience.

What you can do is be empathic. Empathic means that you can reflect the patron's statements back to him, while sympathetic would be sharing those feelings. By acknowledging his feelings, you can let him know they're valid and create a rapport but without becoming personally involved. You keep your professional objectivity, just like other medical professionals and for the same reason.

The patron who comes to a medical library has many issues to deal with besides finding information. He or a loved one may be newly diagnosed or may have a condition that he feels carries a social stigma, like a sexual condition; or the condition may be life changing. Any of those are upsetting, and the patron may have more than one issue to deal with. He may be leery of telling you what he wants or why he wants it or even of asking for your help in finding out what it really is. For that reason, you may get a lot of e-mail questions. The patron may also fear that his information will be shared or made publicly available if he sends his question by e-mail or chat (National Network of Libraries of Medicine 2008).

On the other hand, librarians may be equally leery of telling patrons their findings. The condition may require radical treatment or even be fatal. That's not news that a librarian wants to deliver. Even more disturbing, what if the librarian is wrong? You should tell the patron, though; not to do so would be a form of censorship. What you don't want to do is tell him in your own words since you may have interpreted it badly. You definitely want to print, read, quote, or send the results without commentary.

Confidentiality is a major issue in medical librarianship. The patron may fear that an e-mail could be seen by someone else or, even worse, repeated to someone who works with him (Eberle 2005). Assure the patron that you are aware of his concerns and that information won't be recorded or shared.

Imposed questions are common in health libraries since the real patron may be too ill to come in person. Make sure that you get all the information in the interview right since age and sex are significant variables in some conditions and treatments. Be sure that you give the patron information in a form that he can understand and use, with all the citation information.

The level of information needed is a critical question in this circumstance. Medicine is full of Latin terms, medical terminology, and confusing methodologies.

If the information is too technical to understand, it may be useless. If the information is too simple, it may not meet the needs of a doctor. If the information is too specific to a particular case, it may not apply to your patron's needs. Tell the patron the limits of the information available, show him how to find dictionaries and encyclopedias, and remind him that he can come back for more information later.

Encourage your patrons to make copies that they can take to the doctor. The doctor may or may not be familiar with "that big article in that journal" that the patron tells him about. Having a copy in hand will let the doctor evaluate its applicability.

Be sure that the site your e-mail address is on also has a disclaimer about the limits of your information and services. Be sure you explain it to the patron in person, too, perhaps every time that you quote or recommend a source.

Again, you want a good subject dictionary and perhaps a *Physician's Desk Reference* since many drugs have similar names, as do conditions. Have the patron spell or show you the term that he's asking about.

Tell the patron the limitations of your resources; there may be new treatments or drug trials that aren't in the print sources or not even the online databases yet. Tell him that you can only give him information and that he should discuss it with his doctor.

Once again, you can't make recommendations, even if you have the same condition. You can make wider referrals, though. Medline Plus has local directories, and websites for conditions often have directories of specialists. And once again, you cannot interpret the information for your patron.

When working with medical professionals rather than the public, you can be more proactive. If you are embedded, you will be expected to be more involved. Even if you aren't embedded, you can offer to set up RSS feeds for them, table-of-content alerts, or a blog to alert them to new literature in their specialty or related fields.

You will need to know how to search the databases and possibly synthesize the results into a bibliography or report. That requires a longer and more detailed reference interview than the patron interview, so it's a good idea to have a Web form on your intranet to expedite it. Like the corporate library, speed may be important, but getting the details right is equally so.

Your interview will include questions about the information need in more detail. For instance, does age or sex make a difference? Do other illnesses make a difference? Do previous treatments make a difference in whether the information will be relevant? Some doctors will want everything on the subject, and some will want only what precisely matches their need, so explaining that these questions help you locate what they need will help to move the interview along.

Remember, in a law or medical library, your job is to help the patron find information, but never to interpret it!

REFERENCES

Brown, Karen E., and Beth Lindblom Patkus. "Collections Security: Planning and Prevention for Libraries and Archives." http://www.nedcc.org/resources/leaflets/3Emergency _Management/11CollectionsSecurity.php (accessed July 21, 2010).

Eberle, M. L. "Librarians' Perceptions of the Reference Interview." *Journal of Hospital Librarianship* 5, no. 3 (2005): 29–41.

National Network of Libraries of Medicine. "The Consumer Health Reference Interview and Ethical Issues." http://nnlm.gov/outreach/consumer/ethics.html (accessed June 23, 2010).

ProQuest. "Sample Reference Interview Sheet, Corporate Library." http://www .proquest.asia/assets/downloads/corporate/corp_referenceinterview.doc (accessed July 10, 2010).

FURTHER READING

Allcock, Jana C. "Helping Public Library Patrons Find Medical Information: The Reference Interview." *Public Library Quarterly* 18, no. 33 (2000): 21–27

Arant, Wendi, and Brian Carpenter. "Where is the Line? Legal Reference Service and the Unauthorized Practice of Law (UPL)—Some Guides That Might Help." *Reference & User Services Quarterly* 38 (Spring 1999): 238.

Barclay, Donald, and Deborah Halsted. *The Medical Library Association Consumer Health Reference Service Handbook.* New York: Neal-Schuman, 2001.

Booth, A., A. J. O'Rourke, and N. J. Ford. "Structuring the Pre-Search Reference Interview: A Useful Technique for Handling Clinical Questions." *Bulletin of the Medical Library Association* 88, no. 3 (July 2000): 239–46.

Carson, Bryan M. "Legally Speaking: Reference Questions and the Unauthorized Practice of Law." *Against the Grain*, February 2001, 57–58.

Cohen, Laura B. *Reference Services for Archives and Manuscripts.* Chicago: Society of American Archivists, 1997.

Condon, Charles J. "How to Avoid the Unauthorized Practice of Law at the Reference Desk." *Legal Reference Services Quarterly* 19 (2001): 167.

Duff, W. and A. Fox. " 'You're a Guide Rather Than an Expert': Archival Reference from an Archivist's Point of View." *Journal of the Society of Archivists* 27, no. 2 (2006): 129–53.

Fox, Theodora. "The Lost Art of the Reference Interview." Paper presented at Australian Library and Information Association, 2005. http://conferences.alia.org.au/online2005/ papers/b17.pdf. *The reference interview from the viewpoint of a corporate librarian.*

Francis, Laurie S. "The Genealogy Reference Interview." *PNLA Quarterly* 68, no. 3 (Spring 2004): 13–15.

Gray, John A. "Personal Malpractice Liability of Reference Librarians and Information Brokers." *Journal of Library Administration* 9, no. 2 (1988): 71–83.

Grey, Debbie. "Legal Reference Services: An Annotated Bibliography." *Law Library Journal* 97, no. 3 (2005): 537–64.

Healey, Paul D. "Pro Se Users, Reference Liability, and the Unauthorized Practice of Law: Twenty-Five Selected Readings." *Law Library Journal* 94 (2002): 133–39.

Jacobsen, Phebe R. "The World Upside Down: Reference Priorities and the State Archives." *American Archivist* 44 (Fall 1981): 341–45.

Kepley, Brenda Beasley. "Archives: Accessibility for the Disabled." *American Archivist* 46, no. 1 (Winter 1983): 42–51.

Liebermann, Jana, Arpita Bose, and Gail Kouame. "The Consumer Health Reference Interview and Ethical Issues." http://nnlm.gov/outreach/consumer/ethics.html (accessed September 15, 2010).

Long, Linda J. "Question Negotiation in the Archival Setting: The Use of Interpersonal Communication Techniques in the Reference Interview." *The American Archivist* 52, no. 1 (1989): 40–51.

McMurrer, Nancy, and Cheryl Nyberg. "Legal Reference in Non-Law Libraries." http://lib.law.washington.edu/ref/ppt/handout.pdf (accessed September 12, 2010). Handouts are specific to Washington State. Federal laws are the same around the country. You can use this as a model to make your own handouts for patrons.

Medical Library Association. "Code of Ethics for Health Sciences Librarianship." http://www.mlanet.org/about/ethics.html (accessed September 15, 2010).

National Network of Libraries of Medicine. "Reference Interview Resources." http://nnlm.gov/healthinfoquest/help/interviews.html.

National Network of Libraries of Medicine. "Reference Interview Stages." http://nnlm.gov/healthinfoquest/help/stages.html.

Pugh, Mary Jo. *Providing Reference Services for Archives and Manuscripts.* Chicago: Society of American Archivists, 2005.

Shipton, Clifford K. "The Reference Use of Archives." In *College and University Archives: Selected Readings.* Chicago: Society of American Archivists, 1979.

Simpson, Jack. *Basics of Genealogy Reference: A Librarian's Guide.* Westport, CT: Libraries Unlimited, 2008.

Thomas, Deborah A. "The Consumer Health Reference Interview." *Journal of Hospital Librarianship* 5, no. 2 (2005): 45–56.

Tibbo, Helen R. "Interviewing Techniques for Remote Reference: Electronic versus Traditional Environments." *The American Archivist* 58 (Summer 1995): 294–310.

Tucker, Susan. "Archivists and Genealogical Researchers: A Bibliography." http://www.tulane.edu/~wclib/archivists/archivists.html (accessed July 21, 2010).

Turcotte, Florence. *Public Services in Special Collections.* ARL Spec Kit 296. Washington, D.C.: Association of Research Libraries, 2002.

Whisner, Mary. "Learning from Reference Experience." *Law Library Journal* 102, no. 2 (Spring 2010): 309–14.

Whisner, Mary. *Practicing Reference: Thoughts for Librarians and Legal Researchers.* AALL Publications Series No. 73. Buffalo, NY: Hein, 2006. A compilation of essays published in the *Law Library Journal.*

Wood, M. Sandra, ed. *Medical Librarian 2.0: Use of Web 2.0 Technologies in Reference Services.* Binghamton, NY: Haworth, 2007.

11 I'M ASKING FOR MY . . . CHILD, FRIEND, PARENT, BOSS

Sometimes the patron isn't really the patron. Sometimes the patron is asking someone else's question, called in the literature an "imposed query" (Gross 2001).

The reality is that this is common—more common than you think. Teachers look for books to take to their third-grade class, students look for resources to satisfy their teacher, and people look for books for their discussion group. Maybe the child reads English, but the parent doesn't. All these are "looking for someone else."

You don't get to ask why the real patron isn't there. Maybe the child has chickenpox, maybe the husband is working, maybe the aunt is disabled, and maybe the boss treats his employees like slaves. It's not your business; your business is making the best of a bad reference interview.

It's a bad situation because the asking patron doesn't always know what the other person wants. It's like buying clothes for someone else: the salesperson will ask a lot of questions that you may not know the answer to. What size? What color? What age? What style? If you don't know the answers, the odds are that the person the clothes are for won't be able to use them.

It's the same with reference questions. You need to ask questions to find a good match that will satisfy the patron's needs.

Sometimes it's like playing telephone as a child, passing the message along and seeing how it changes. The teacher may say, "Write a report on the history of New Mexico," the child tells the parent it's about Mexico and all that new stuff, and the parent tells the librarian it's about political changes in Central America.

Often, the asking party is a parent, asking for a child, even if the child is there with him. The parent may be there to help the child express his needs, to see that he gets appropriate materials, or to make sure he isn't ignored by the librarian. Still, the real patron is the child. You want to ask the child the questions, even if the parent answers for them (Brown 2010).

To talk to the real patron, you can find something for the parent to do. Ask them to look at encyclopedias or current journal indexes, something that's possibly helpful but mostly gives the child a chance to speak for himself. Often the child has a better understanding of what he wants and other ideas than the parent. Universities aren't the only place that has "helicopter parents," who hover around the student and oversee everything they do. Younger children are less likely than college students to tell their parents to land somewhere else, so you may have to do that for them.

The opposite case is also true. Often, a child has been in school and learned English quicker than the parent or neighbor they are with. They are interpreters and sometimes filters for their information needs. Children may not always pass on all the information you give them, either because they don't understand it or, in the case of teens, because they don't agree with it.

It's an embarrassing situation for the adult, so be sensitive to the real patron's feelings. Talk to him as the patron, but you might want to be a little more formal than you are normally. Children may refer to him as "Papa"; you can ask how he would like to be addressed in your first exchange. That both recognizes that he is the patron and gives him some of the dignity he may feel he has lost depending on a child.

Focus on the patron's need and not the child's presence. You can thank the child for his help at the end of the interview, but don't make it a part of the actual interview. Pay attention to the patron's body language. If he shows signs of being frustrated and uncomfortable, you aren't communicating, and it may be time to bring in another translator. Ask his permission to do so and apologize for your lack of language skills. That keeps him in control of the interview and shows respect for his language skills. The adult saves face, and it doesn't cost you any. Explain the interview thus far to the new translator and continue. The child may still want to be part of the process, so you can include him by asking him to get materials you have identified.

If the real patron who will use the information is a student, you can ask for a copy of the assignment and add it to your wiki or file. That works better for elementary students and parents; it may not exist for college students who get their assignments orally. You may need to summarize it yourself or call the instructor.

Younger students may be and almost certainly are looking in a field they don't know and have a hard time putting their needs into words. A student studying Germany for the first time may not realize that there were two Germanys for a while or that there used to be kings there or many other things that adults assume are common knowledge. They're not common to an eight-year-old. Parents my not realize that either and frame their question in a way that doesn't help the child.

Let the child have as much input as he can give and talk only to the child. If the parent thinks the child is getting things wrong, he will chime in, but keep your attention on the child. Children are very likely to give you nonverbal clues like rolling their eyes or nodding, so stay alert for them.

HOMESCHOOLERS

Homeschoolers are both primary users and second-party patrons. They often look for books that they can use as texts and reference books. While it is rare that they are able to check out what we refer to as "reference books," younger children can use one or two books for their work, while the parent can find books in the adult section. Homeschoolers will be frequent visitors for children's programming and story hours, and offering a room for them to meet is good public relations. It also allows the child to browse the collections for himself and ask his own questions.

You can help homeschoolers by having a section for homeschooling materials and subject displays that they can choose from. Since homeschoolers are creating their own lessons, they may be very heavy library users; making life easier for them will keep them coming. Websites and handouts with sources for each grade, state regulations on homeschooling, and lists of local museums, historic homes, and businesses that offer tours will be appreciated.

When interviewing homeschoolers, you need to remember that they are asking for two: as both the teacher and the student. If the parent focuses on adult sources, ask if he needs a children's book also and vice versa. If the child is there, include him in the interview or do a separate one after talking to the parent. Ignoring what a child wants and looking for what a parent needs instead may explain why people don't ask librarians for help later in life. You can always do both.

Children will sometimes look for materials for classmates' projects—just because. A child who can find his way around a library is often considered an expert by his peers. That's true of older students, too; many high school and college classes have a resident library expert who other students will look to. Research says that people turn to peers before librarians; this is a case where the student does know more about the assignment but seldom as much as a librarian about the resources. The student is more accessible, though: there in the classroom, after class, or on Facebook.

That happens with adults, too. People will often ask for materials for a family member or friend, just because it's on their mind. If the patron's brother is newly diagnosed with diabetes or his sister is having triplets, he may be responding more to his own needs than his family member or friend's real need, but it's a good impulse, and you can offer both kinds of materials.

If you work in a college, you can ask teachers to send you copies of the assignment before the term, but often they want the students to negotiate the library themselves. Those are the people who want "satisficing" answers, ones that are "good enough" for the assignment. Students don't have a real interest in imposed queries that they have no stake in—at any age.

Professors sometimes tell students they can't use anything they find online, confusing the students about what they can use. Can they use subscription databases? Google Scholar to find articles? Government sites? The answer is sometimes "no." Not all professors understand the difference between databases and the Web or understand that we don't subscribe to all paper journals. Be brave and call him. You can explain that the assignment is confusing both you and his students and explain the confusion about online and subscription sources. He may still want the students to use all print sources, and that's okay. Say good-bye with an invitation to come to the library for a cup of coffee. You've made a connection with a faculty member, and that's a good thing.

Looking for the boss (or any other business question) should bring some questions to your mind right away. How soon do you need it, how recent does it have to be, and how much do you need? The first answer to the first question will almost always be "now." Probe further—within the hour, the day, the week? The answer to the second will be "today"; ask if this month or year is close enough. The third one will almost always be "everything." Unless they ask about vegan leopards, you'll need to narrow that down a lot. This is where knowing the end use will be a big help. If the answer is to illustrate an ad for Big Purple Monkey shampoo, you'll know to look at graphics and to ask the public-domain-versus-license question.

If you have a Web form for remote users, suggest to for-my-boss users that their boss fill it out since he's the one with the answers. That may not always be possible. The boss may regard it as the employee's job, and the employee may have more than face to save. In that case, ask the employee everything you can think of to give you clues. Are there any big projects in the works? What led to his being sent? Does he have any special knowledge that the boss thought would be useful in finding the information? Is the deadline significant, such as right before a big presentation? Is there a big event coming up?

As a medical, law, or corporate librarian, you may be the one doing the searching for the boss. You will also get other types of second-party questions, and it may be difficult to remember which ones are from the boss and which are from other patrons, but for confidentiality's sake, you have to do so.

There is still another class of third-party reference question, that is, when one librarian asks another for his expertise. That can happen when the second librarian has specialized knowledge and collaborates on an answer or when the patron is referred to another librarian or library (Pomerantz 2008).

The phone may be old technology, but it can be your best ally. Knowing who to call for an answer or who may have the best resources to find it can save you and your patron time. Librarians share a language (their jargon can confuse patrons) and can state their need specifically, consulting with the patron when clarification is needed or just handing the phone over once they've concluded that their part of the transaction is done. It's important and just polite to confirm that you've reached the right party and to tell them what you already know and have found.

It's common for questions that have led to a dead end to appear on listservs. Besides the Stumpers list, searches for primary sources also appear on the Archives and Archivists list. It may be more appropriate to send them to a subject-oriented list, such as an art or a history list. The subscribers may not be librarians, but they are well versed in the field and have specialized knowledge and sometimes rare resources they can consult.

Many listservs require the poster to register, so many questions are posted by a librarian who is a member rather than the original patron. Where the question came as an e-mail, it is often forwarded as is; when it is the result of a reference interview, it is summary of it. These questions also show that reference librarians are not immune to the problems they themselves deal with every day: incomplete information or questions, a lack of what has already been located, and reply information.

Sample Interviews

Do you have any books about poetry?

Do you want a book of poems or something about poetry in general?

Both, I guess. But they have to be Spanish.

Can you tell me more about what you need them for? That will help me find something useful.

Well, it's for my son. He's in college, but he says there's no good books there. He has to find five poets and write about them.

Can you tell me anything about the class?

It's his English class, so I don't know why they have to be in Spanish. He says he has to tell why they write differently, like writing in Spanish isn't different enough?

Do the poems have to be in Spanish, or do the poets have to be from Spanish-speaking country?

I don't know. He said they don't have anything at the college.

How soon does he need the information?

I guess really soon. He's been looking online for a couple weeks, he says.

Okay, he needs something about Spanish poets and their writings to write for his English class? First we're going to look for a book on Spanish poets and Spanish-speaking poets to find a list of Spanish poets and then look for them by name. What college does he go to? I can search their catalog and see if there's something he overlooked there as well.

I need some books on that big explosion last month.

There aren't any books on it yet; it's only been a few weeks. There's a lot of coverage in the newspapers and magazines, though. Have you looked at any of those?

He says he has to have books. He says he can't use anything from the Web, either.

You're looking for someone else, then . . .

For my son. His physics teacher says they have to have books about it.

What does the teacher want them to do with what they find?

They have to write a paper on why it happened and why it's so dangerous.

Okay, you're talking about the oil refinery explosion? So he needs something on why oil refineries are dangerous and about the recent accident?

Yeah, but it has to be from books.

Let's start with encyclopedias, then. That will give some background. You can't check out encyclopedias, though. Can your son come in and look at them?

I guess, I just told him I'd get the books while I was out.

Let's look at the catalog and see what's there. That might give him some background, but they won't have anything on that particular explosion yet. That will have to come from newspapers and magazines. We do have some books on older accidents; will those work?

I don't know; I just know what he told me. He really wants to do it about that accident.

Here are the older books. If he comes in to look at the encyclopedias, he can check the newspapers then. When is his paper due?

Tomorrow. Can I just photocopy all that stuff?

Yes, you can copy from the encyclopedias and newspapers and check these books out. We close at six today, so if he has any more questions, he'll have to come in before then. Do you think this is enough information?

I don't know. Can he call you if it isn't?

He can, here's the phone number. It would be good if he called and we could talk; that would be faster since he'll have to get anything from here before six. Do you have any more questions?

REFERENCES

Brown, Anita. "Reference Services for Children: Information Needs and Wants in the Public Library." http://www.alia.org.au/publishing/alj/53.3/full.text/brown.html (accessed September 15, 2010).

Gross, Melissa. "Imposed Information Seeking in Public Libraries and School Library Media Centres: A Common Behaviour?" *Information Research* 6, no. 2 (2001). http://InformationR.net/ir/6-2/paper100.html (accessed September 15, 2010).

Pomerantz, Jeffrey. "Collaboration as the Norm in Reference Work." *Reference & User Services Quarterly* 46, no. 1 (2008): Features. http://www.rusq.org/2008/01/05/collaboration-as-the-norm-in-reference-work (accessed October 1, 2010).

FURTHER READINGS

Chu, Clara. "Immigrant Children Mediators (ICM): Bridging the Literacy Gap in Immigrant Communities." *The New Review of Children's Literature and Librarianship* 5 (1999): 85–94.

Gross, Melissa. "The Imposed Query." *RQ* 35, no. 2 (1995): 236–43.

Gross, Melissa. "The Imposed Query and Information Services for Children." *Journal of Youth Services in Libraries* 12, no. 2 (2000): 10–17.

Gross, Melissa. *Studying Children's Questions: Imposed and Self-Generated Information Seeking at School.* Lanham, MD: Scarecrow Press, 2006.

Kaplan, P. "Reaching Out to Homeschooling Families: Services and Programs." *Illinois Libraries* 1 (2001): 44–46.

Kleist-Tesch, J. M. "Homeschoolers and the Public Library." *Journal of Youth Services in Libraries* 3 (1998): 231–41.

Klipsch, P. R. "An Educated Collection for Homeschoolers." *Library Journal* 120, no. 2 (1995): 47–50.

Lerch, M. T., and J. Welch. *Serving Homeschooled Teens and Their Parents.* Westport, CT: Libraries Unlimited, 2004.

McCarthy, A., and D. L. Andersen. "Homeschoolers at the Public Library: Are Library Services and Policies Keeping Pace?" *Journal of the Library Administration and Management Section* 3, no. 1 (2006–2007): 5–44.

Moore, P., and A. St. George. "Children as Information Seekers: The Cognitive Demands of Books and Library Systems." *School Library Media Quarterly* Spring (1999): 161–68.

Scheps, S. G. "Homeschoolers in the Library." *School Library Journal* 2 (1999): 38–39.

Scheps, S. G. *The Librarian's Guide to Homeschooling Resources.* Chicago: American Library Association, 1998.

Slattery, A. "In a Class of Their Own: As More Families Turn to Homeschooling, Public Libraries Can Be an Invaluable Resource." *School Library Journal* 8 (2005): 44–46.

INDEX

INDEX

ABOUT THE AUTHOR

SUSAN KNOER teaches a reference class online for the University of Kentucky in Lexington, where she earned her MLS. She was photographic editor for *Law at the Falls*.